Memorizing God's Word: ™ HIStory (NKJV)

Seeing Jesus in Genesis Chapter One

R. M. Lewis

WestBow
PRESS
A DIVISION OF THOMAS NELSON

WestBow Press books may be ordered through booksellers or by contacting:

WestBow Press
A Division of Thomas Nelson
1663 Liberty Drive
Bloomington, IN 47403
www.westbowpress.com
1-(866) 928-1240

ISBN: 978-1-4497-1502-1 (sc)

Library of Congress Cataloguing-in-Publication Data 2011925479

Printed in the United States of America

WestBow Press rev. date: 3/23/2011

This book is dedicated to all the pastors and Bible teachers in my life from infancy.

It also is dedicated to publishers who meticulously preserve the sacred trust of word for word translations of the Holy Bible from reliable copies of ancient manuscripts. Without word for word translations, I could not have written this book.

A special thank you to Joyce Strickland and Janet Norman for editorial services.

I thank my family and my prayer partner – best friends who enrich my life with prayer, support, and joy.

To my prayer partner – best friends, what a joyous time being with you at my 40th wedding anniversary! Some of you were present for the 25th celebration, but this time was exceptional with the effort of country-wide travel and your wonderful testimonies enjoyed by so many loved ones.

Above all my love, devotion, and adulation to my Savior and Lord Jesus Christ for without abiding in You, I am nothing.

CONTENTS
New King James Version

I.   Seeing Jesus in Creation   9
     A.   The Quest   9
     B.   Creator God   11

II. Demonstrating the FLOW Coding Method ®   13

III. Memorizing Tips   15

IV. Mastering Long Passages   17

V.   Practicing What You Have Learned   19

VI. Resource of FLOW Coded™ Scriptures: Overviews   23
     A.   FLOW   23
     B.   Analogy   25

VII. Resource of Scriptures: Seeing Jesus in Creation   27
     A.   Day 1: Knowing Him / Foundation   27
     B.   Day 2: Saving Faith / Salvation   39
     C.   Day 3: Standing Secure / Assurance   59
     D.   Day 4: Becoming Christlike / Transformation   71
     E.   Day 5: Glorifying God / Maturation   85
     F.   Day 6: Anticipating Heaven / Kingdom   101
     G.   Day 7: Living Hope / Meditation   121

     Epilogue: The Essentials   129
          How to Be Saved / Receive Christ in Your Heart   129
          Lordship: Two Greatest Commandments   129
          The Holy Bible: The Living Word of God   129

I.   SEEING JESUS IN CREATION: THE QUEST

My fascination with "Seeing Jesus in Creation" began more than twelve years ago. It began with a question of why did God bless the entirety of Creation as "good," but did not include "it was good" on the second day.

I read other reliable word for word Bible translations and "good" was definitely not there for Creation Day Two. It was also noteworthy that "the light" on Creation Day One was different from the "lights made" on Creation Day Four.

My curiosity was energized as to why? Was there an analogy related to the omission of "good" on the second day, and the distinction between the light on the first day of Creation and the lights on Day Four? Those two facts were so exciting to ponder as I read the Bible and listened to Scripture.

I made an elementary sketch of the days of Creation early one morning, because after midnight I would study the Bible and meditate. That was my time with God in silence without interruption.

Subsequent drawings were made after my first one shredded from frequent use. The date of a later sketch is January 12, 1999.

When a particular Scripture was illuminated, I would be ecstatic. Scripture references, notes, and additional details would be added to the sketch.

It seemed reasonable that if there was an analogy, it could only be about the ministry of Jesus. My mind was intrigued with the hope of seeing Jesus in Creation.

The quest was on with exuberance. My lifestyle of reading the Bible from cover to cover took on a new intensity as I searched for Jesus. The front cover of this book is designed from the old drawings from 1999.

The collection of Bible verses in this book represent more than a decade of pondering with God usually between the hours of 1:30 a.m. to 3:30 a.m. and/or 3:00 a.m. to 5:00 a.m. This was supreme private time with God, and it still thrills me.

"Seeing Jesus in Creation" is an analogy; it is not theological doctrine. It is merely my perspective of viewing Scriptures about Jesus and the church through the narrative of Genesis Chapter One.

This book has a dual purpose. My first purpose is to share some interesting insights from God's work in Creation and Jesus' work on earth. My second purpose is to demonstrate the FLOW Coding Method ® for memorizing God's Word.

My hope is that you enjoy the scriptural narrative about Jesus Christ which dovetails Bible verses from Genesis Chapter One into a synopsis of HIStory. After reading the next page, please proceed to page 25, the Analogy Overview.

Back pages are intentionally left blank except for analogy pages.

Seeing Jesus in Creation: Creator God

Is it possible to see the Lord Jesus Christ in Genesis Chapter One? Are there Bible verses about the earthly ministry of Jesus Christ that could be interwoven into Days One through Seven?

The Holy Bible from Genesis to Revelation declares HIStory, but in particular in Genesis Chapter One, there are dovetailing Bible verses for:

Day 1: Knowing Him / Foundation
Day 2: Saving Faith / Salvation
Day 3: Standing Secure / Assurance
Day 4: Becoming Christlike / Transformation
Day 5: Glorifying God / Maturation
Day 6: Anticipating Heaven / Kingdom, and
Day 7: Living Hope / Meditation.

"The Quest" on page 9 summarizes how this search began. The analogy of Genesis Chapter One, "Seeing Jesus in Creation," is in the Resource of Scriptures. It begins on page 25. The Holy Bible declares:

1. The Word was with God, and the Word was God. He [Jesus] was in the beginning with God.   John 1:1b,2

2. And He is before all things, and in Him all things consist.   Col. 1:17

3. For by Him all things were created that are in heaven and that are on earth, visible and invisible, whether thrones or dominions or principalities or powers. All things were created through Him and for Him. Col. 1:16

4. And He is the head of the body, the church... that in all things He may have the preeminence.   Col. 1:18

5. All things were made through Him, and without Him nothing was made that was made.   John 1:3

6. For it pleased the Father that in Him [Jesus] all the fullness should dwell, and by Him to reconcile all things to Himself ... whether things on earth or things in heaven, having made peace through the blood of His cross.   Col. 1:19,20

7. In this the love of God was manifested toward us, that God has sent His only begotten Son [Jesus] into the world, that we might live through Him.   1 John 4:9

8. For He made Him who knew no sin to be sin for us, that we might become the righteousness of God in Him.   2 Cor. 5:21

9. For there is one God and one Mediator between God and men, the Man Christ Jesus, who gave Himself a ransom for all, to be testified in due time ...   1 Tim. 2:5,6

The tool for memorizing Scriptures of HIStory in this book, is the FLOW Coding Method ®. This system is an easy tool that immediately and successfully works. It is basically a two-part process: (1) visualizing a Bible verse in phrases, and (2) Coding or writing the first letter of each word in the phrase. "**FLOW**" is an acronym for:

> *F*irst
> *L*etter
> *O*f
> *W*ord™.

This book explains in detail how to use the FLOW Method™. Depending on the verse, an already coded Bible verse takes five minutes to memorize. Once memorized, the Holy Spirit can illuminate that Scripture in your heart at anytime. **Please proceed to page 25, the Analogy Overview.**

II. DEMONSTRATING THE FLOW CODING METHOD ®
The Nine Steps

1. **Ask God to help you.**
Pray for His help in understanding and in memorizing the Scripture.

2. **Read aloud the verse.**
Use your senses of **seeing, speaking,** and **hearing** to stimulate your memory.

Unformatted Verse Example:
John 3:17
For God did not send His Son into the world to condemn the world, but that the world through Him might be saved.

3. **Visualize writing the verse in phrases using a separate line for each phrase.**
Observe how to divide the verse into short, comfortable phrases.

4. **Write the verse in Phrase-format with its address before and after the verse.**
A verse can be formatted into phrases by concepts, natural pauses of thought, punctuation, and by placing difficult to remember words on a separate line.

> **Phrase-formatted Verse Example:**
> John 3:17
> For God did not send
> His Son into the world
> to condemn the world,   but that
> the world through Him
> might be saved.
> John 3:17

5. **Code the Phrase-formatted verse by writing the first letter of each word.**
FLOW is the acronym for Coding or writing the *F*irst *L*etter *O*f each *W*ord.

Leave a blank line to prompt your memory for the second address or reference.

> **FLOW Coded Verse Example:**
> John 3:17
> F G d n s
> H S i t w
> t c t w, b t
> t w t H
> m b s.
> Address____

6. **Read aloud the Phrase-formatted verse with its address three or more times. PAUSE after each line.**
Read with emphasis or repeat a difficult to remember phrase three times. For example, read aloud three times:
" ... to condemn the world,   but that ... "

7. **Use the Code to say aloud the verse with its address three or more times.**
Repeat difficult lines three or more times. Look back at the words as needed. If you keep forgetting certain words, re-read aloud the Phrase-formatted verse several times before using the Code again. For example:
> John 3:17
> F G d n s   (recite with emphasis)
> H S i t w   (recite with emphasis)
> t c t w, b t (repeat three times)
> t w t H   (recite with emphasis)
> m b s.   (recite with emphasis)
> Address____

8. **Recite aloud the verse from memory while visualizing the Code.**

9. **Thank God for helping you. Review often with the Code first, then the verse.**

III.   MEMORIZING TIPS

1. If a verse is already Phrase-formatted™ and Coded, use a half sheet of paper to cover the Code, or glue the verse to an index card, and use the reverse side for the Code. **Read the verse out loud three times. Pause after each line**.

2. When Phrase-formatting™ a verse, use large type, and write the Scripture reference or address before and after the verse(s). Read aloud the reference/address each time.

3. When Coding a verse, leave the second address line blank to prompt your memory for the reference. Say the reference out loud.

4. When memorizing consecutive verses, write the reference number beside each verse if you like.

5. As needed, also number the lines (1, 2, 3, etc.) to prevent skipping a line as you practice.

6. When Phrase-formatting™, look for patterns in a verse, for example, repeated concepts, words, parts of speech, etc.

7. Experiment with memory prompts: spacial alignments within a line, indentation for various parts of speech, italics, color-coding, bold print, and underlining.

8. If a verse is difficult to remember, Phrase-format™ the Scripture with more memory prompts. Also in rapid succession, repeat three times or recite with emphasis any forgotten line. As you use the FLOW Coding Method ®, customize your prompts.

9. Memory prompts that can be used to enhance memorization are: shorter Phrase-formatted™ lines and spacial alignments.

10. If a Bible translation does not capitalize the pronouns referring to God, consider bold print, underlining, or color-coding **His** pronouns to increase comprehension.

11. At the end of a line if you triple space before the conjunction "and" as well as the pronoun "that", it will prompt your memory for the next word. The same could be done for other conjunctions if you so desire.

12. Possessive words could be coded with 's. For example, "those who are Christ's" is coded as "t w a C's." Keep the punctuation of hyphens and dashes. For example, "I – My" is coded as "I – M."

Isaiah 45:12a	Is. 45:12a
I have made the earth, And	I h m t e, A
created man on it.	c m o i.
I – My hands –	I – M h –
stretched out	s o
the heavens,	t h,
Is. 45:12a	Addr._____

13. To enhance retention, observe the first word of each Phrase-formatted™ line, and read aloud three times the sequence of first words. Please refer to the verse above and speak: **I, created, I – My, stretched, the.** Now read the Phrase-formatted™ verse.

14. When reading or reciting Bible verses, remember to: **Speak out loud at least three times, and PAUSE after each line.**

IV.   MASTERING LONG PASSAGES

1. Read aloud the entire passage of Bible verses for understanding.

2. Re-read aloud the passage noting the natural flow of concepts, words, and parts of speech for Phrase-formatting™ the verses. If possible, use only one line for each verse.

3. Divide the passage into groups of verses. Memorize one group then recite from the beginning before memorizing the next group.

4. Consider using bold print, underlining, or color-coding for references to God. For example: "**to the Lord**" and "**His name.**"

5. Use *italics* for verbs. This will prompt your memory that a *verb* comes next.

6. With a lengthy passage, use additional lines and spaces only as needed. Write the reference number beside each Bible verse. **Read out loud. PAUSE after each line.**

7. When a verse is difficult to remember, practice repeating three times and/or reciting with emphasis a line. For example:

Isaiah 45:18
For thus says the LORD,	(with emphasis)
Who created the heavens,	(with emphasis)
Who is God,	(with emphasis)
Who formed the earth ...	(repeat three times)
I am the LORD, and	(with emphasis)
there is no other.	(repeat three times)
Is. 45:18	

Isaiah 45:18
F t s t L,	(with emphasis)
W c t h,	(with emphasis)
W i G,	(with emphasis)
W f t e ...	(repeat three times)
I a t L, a	(with emphasis)
t i n o.	(repeat three times)
Address____	

8. Create a Memory Barcode prompt at the top of long passages. Please refer to below and "Practicing What You Have Learned."

Memory Barcode™ Phrase-formatted Example

Note: At the top of the group of verses below is a Memory Barcode; it lists verse reference numbers **6,7**, and **8**, and the first letter of each verse and its subordinate line(s). The Scripture below is formatted to have references to **God in bold print**, and *verbs* and some *adverbs* in *italics*. The letters in the Memory Barcode retain the capitalization, bold print, and italics of the first letter of each line. (Psalm 33:6-14 is on page 21.)

Psalm 33:6-8	**FLOW Coded™**
6 7 8	**6 7 8**
BA HH *LL*	**BA HH** *LL*
6 **By the word of the LORD** the heavens *were made,*	6 **B t w o t L** t h *w m,*
And all the host of them **by the breath of His mouth.**	A a t h o t **b t b o H m.**
7 **He** *gathers* the waters of the sea together as a heap;	7 **H** *g* t w o t s t a a h;
He *lays up* the deep in storehouses.	**H** *l u* t d i s.
8 *Let* all the earth *fear* **the LORD**;	8 *L* a t e *f* t **L**;
Let all the inhabitants of the world *stand* **in awe of Him.**	*L* a t i o t w *s* i a o **H.**

V. PRACTICING WHAT YOU HAVE LEARNED
(Be **doers** of the 9 Steps)

A. SHORT VERSE UNFORMATTED EXAMPLE:
He is the image of the invisible God, the firstborn over all creation.   Colossians 1:15

Phrase-formatted™	**FLOW Coded**™
Colossians 1:15	Colossians 1:15
[Jesus] He is the image	H i t i
of the invisible God,	o t i G,
the firstborn over all creation.	t f o a c.
Col. 1:15	Addr.____

B. MORE DIFFICULT VERSE UNFORMATTED EXAMPLE:
For since the creation of the world His invisible attributes are clearly seen, being understood by the things that are made, even His eternal power and Godhead, so that they are without excuse, Rom.1:20

Phrase-formatted™ by Punctuation	**FLOW Coded**™
Romans 1:20	Romans 1:20
For since the creation of the world His invisible attributes are clearly seen,	F s t c o t w H i a a c s,
being understood by the things that are made,	b u b t t t a m,
even His eternal power and Godhead,	e H e p a G,
so that they are without excuse,	s t t a w e,
Rom. 1:20	Addr.____

Phrase-formatted™ by Thought Pauses	**FLOW Coded**™
Romans 1:20	Romans 1:20
For since the creation of the world	F s t c o t w
His invisible attributes are clearly seen,	H i a a c s,
being understood by the things that are made,	b u b t t t a m,
even His eternal power and Godhead,	e H e p a G,
so that they are without excuse,	s t t a w e,
Rom. 1:20	Addr.____

Phrase-formatted™ with Memory Prompts		**FLOW Coded**™	
Romans 1:20		Romans 1:20	
For since the creation of the world		F s t c o t w	
His invisible attributes		H i a	
are clearly seen,		a c s,	
being understood by the things	that	b u b t t	t
are made,		a m,	
even His eternal power	and	e H e p	a
Godhead,	so that	G,	s t
they are without excuse,		t a w e,	
Rom. 1:20		Addr.____	

Practicing What You Have Learned
(Be **doers** of the 9 Steps)

C. LONG PASSAGE UNFORMATTED EXAMPLE:

Psalm 33:6-14

6 By the word of the LORD the heavens were made,
And all the host of them by the breath of His mouth.
7 He gathers the waters of the sea together as a heap;
He lays up the deep in storehouses.
8 Let all the earth fear the LORD;
Let all the inhabitants of the world stand in awe of Him.
9 For He spoke, and it was done;
He commanded, and it stood fast.
10 The LORD brings the counsel of the nations to
nothing; He makes the plans of the peoples of no effect.

11 The counsel of the LORD stands forever,
The plans of His heart to all generations.
12 Blessed is the nation whose God is the LORD, The people He has chosen as His own inheritance.
13 The LORD looks from heaven;
He sees all the sons of men.
14 From the place of His dwelling He looks
On all the inhabitants of the earth;

Memory Barcode™ Phrase-formatted Passage
Psalm 33:6-14

6	7	8	9	10	11	12	13	14
BA	HH	*LL*	FH	TH	TT	BT	TH	FO

6 **By the word of the LORD** the heavens *were made,*
   And all the host of them **by the breath of His mouth.**
7 **He** *gathers* the waters of the sea together as a heap;
   He *lays up* the deep in storehouses.

8 *Let* all the earth *fear* **the LORD;**
   Let all the inhabitants of the world *stand* **in awe of Him.**
9 For **He** *spoke,* and it *was done;*
   He *commanded,* and it *stood* fast.

10 **The LORD** *brings* the counsel of the nations to nothing;
   He *makes* the plans of the peoples of no effect.
11 **The counsel of the LORD** *stands* forever,
   The plans of His heart to all generations.
12 Blessed *is* the nation **whose God** *is* **the LORD,**
   The people **He** *has chosen* **as His own inheritance.**

13 **The LORD** *looks* from heaven;
   He *sees* all the sons of men.
14 **From the place of His dwelling He** *looks*
   On all the inhabitants of the earth;
   Ps. 33:6-14

FLOW Coded™
Psalm 33:6-14

6	7	8	9	10	11	12	13	14
BA	HH	*LL*	FH	TH	TT	BT	TH	FO

6 **B t w o t L** t h w *m,*
   A a t h o t **b t b o H m.**
7 **H** *g* t w o t s t a a h;
   H *l* u t d i s.

8 *L* a t e *f* t **L;**
   L a t i o t w s i a o **H.**
9 F **H** *s,* a i w *d;*
   H *c,* a i s f.

10 **T L** *b* t c o t n t n;
   H *m* t p o t p o n e.
11 **T c o t L** *s* f,
   T p o H h t a g.
12 B *i* t n w **G** *i* t **L,**
   T p **H** *h c a* **H o i.**

13 **T L** *l* f h;
   H *s* a t s o m.
14 **F t p o H d H** *l*
   O a t i o t e;
   Addr._____

FLOW OVERVIEW

The Scriptures in this section are a narrative of God's work at Creation and Christ's work on earth. The Bible verses are formatted for memorization using the FLOW Coding Method ®.

In this Resource of FLOW Coded™ Scriptures, the Scriptures for each day of Creation are interwoven with corresponding Bible verses. For the pure delight of the Word of God, first read the Scriptures, then experiment with the method.

Effective helps and suggestions for using the method are included in the chapters on: Demonstrating the FLOW Coding Method ®; Memorizing Tips; Mastering Long Passages; and Practicing What You Have Learned.

If you follow the instructions in the above sections, you have the tools to implement the FLOW Method™ and to enjoy how it works. There is no exact way of using the technique. If you have a better method of coding Scripture, use it.

After reading the Resource of Scriptures section, select your own verses to be memorized. For a quick start, use a half sheet of paper to cover the Code, or fold a two-column page in this section of the book and begin practicing. You will enjoy the results.

ANALOGY OVERVIEW

Analogy: a partial likeness between two things that are compared. The following analogies view the Scriptures about Jesus and the church through Genesis Chapter One. The first page of each Analogy is the synopsis. The second page is the Genesis account for that day of Creation and the correlation. The pages following the Analogy have corresponding Bible verses interwoven with the Genesis account. I have highlighted, "God said that it was good."

Creation	God's Work at Creation	Jesus' Work on Earth	Analogy
DAY 1	The Light	Incarnation	Page 27, 28
DAY 2	Firmament / Expanse	Crucifixion	Page 39, 40
DAY 3	Earth and Vegetation	Burial and Resurrection	Page 59, 60
DAY 4	Lights	Witnesses	Page 71, 72
DAY 5	Fish and Birds	Great Commission and Pentecost	Page 85, 86
DAY 6	Adam and His Bride	Christ and His Bride	Page 101, 102
DAY 7	God Rested	Jesus Christ Rested	Page 121, 122

DAY ONE: ANALOGY SYNOPSIS

On Creation Day One,
God's work in Creation was to send a unique light.

This reminds me of God the Father sending Jesus,
the true Light to the world.

ANALOGY: CREATION DAY ONE

Analogy: a partial likeness between two things that are compared. This analogy seeks to view the Scriptures about Jesus and the church through the narrative of Genesis Chapter One.

Creation Day 1: Genesis 1:1-5

1 In the beginning God created the heavens and the earth. 2 The earth was without form, and void; and darkness was on the face of the deep. And the Spirit of God was hovering over the face of the waters. 3 Then God said, "Let there be light"; and there was light. 4 And God saw the light, that it was good; and God divided the light from the darkness. 5 God called the light Day, and the darkness He called Night. So the evening and the morning were the first day.

God's Work in Creation: God said, "Let there be light." Light is given or sent.

Jesus' Work on Earth: Incarnation: God the Father gave Jesus, the true Light, to the world.

Bible Verse Keywords: Light; true Light; life; I must work; morning star; the Bright and Morning Star; Light has dawned; And God saw the light, that it was good;

Pondered: 1. The Holy Bible is replete with Scriptures proclaiming that the world was made "by", "for", "in", and "through" Jesus Christ. Please refer to "Seeing Jesus in Creation: Creator God" on page 11.

2. The lights on Creation Day Four are made. Note the distinction between the "made lights" on Creation Day Four from "the light" on Day One.
Creation Day Four:
Genesis 1:14 Then God said, "Let there be lights in the firmament of the heavens to divide the day from the night; and let them be for signs and seasons, and for days and years; 15 and let them be for lights in the firmament of the heavens to give light on the earth"; and it was so. 16 Then God made two great lights: the greater light to rule the day, and the lesser light to rule the night. He made the stars also. 17 God set them in the firmament of the heavens to give light on the earth, 18 and to rule over the day and over the night, and to divide the light from the darkness. And God saw that it was good. 19 So the evening and the morning were the fourth day.

Creation Day One:
Genesis 1:3 Then God said, "Let there be light"; and there was light.
4 And God saw the light, that it was good; and God divided the light from the darkness. 5 God called the light Day, and the darkness He called Night. So the evening and the morning were the first day.

3. On Creation Days Three through Six, the Bible declares, "And God saw that it was good." Only on Creation Day One, does God identify "it." The Scripture heralds, "And God saw the light, that it was good ... ."

4. Could it be that this unique "light" is an analogy of Jesus, the "true Light," the beloved Son of God, in Whom Father God is well pleased?

DAY 1:   KNOWING HIM

FOUNDATION SCRIPTURES

1.   Genesis 1:1,2
In the beginning God created
the heavens   and the earth.
The earth was without form, and
void;   and darkness was
on the face of the deep.   And
the Spirit of God   was hovering
over the face of the waters.
Gen. 1:1,2

1.   Genesis 1:1,2
I t b G c
t h   a t e.
T e w w f,   a
v;   a d w
o t f o t d.   A
t S o G   w h
o t f o t w.
Addr.____

2.   Genesis 1:3
Then God said,
Let there be light;   and
there was light.
Gen. 1:3

2.   Genesis 1:3
T G s,
L t b l;   a
t w l.
Addr.____

3.   John 1:9
That was the true Light [Jesus]
which gives light
to every man
coming into the world.
Jn. 1:9

3.   John 1:9
T w t t L
w g l
t e m
c i t w.
Addr.____

4.   John 3:16
For God so loved the world   that
He gave
His only begotten Son,   that
whoever believes in Him [Jesus]
should not perish,   but
have everlasting life.
Jn. 3:16

4.   John 3:16
F G s l t w t
H g
H o b S,   t
w b i H
s n p,   b
h e l.
Addr.____

5.   1 Thessalonians 5:9
For God did not appoint us
to wrath,   but
to obtain salvation
through
our Lord Jesus Christ,
1 Thess. 5:9

5.   1 Thessalonians 5:9
F G d n a u
t w,   b
t o s
t
o L J C,
Addr.____

6.   Acts 4:12
Nor is there salvation
in any other,
for there is no other name
under heaven ...
by which we must be saved.
Acts 4:12

6.   Acts 4:12
N i t s
i a o,
f t i n o n
u h ...
b w w m b s.
Addr._____

7.   Hebrews 2:14
Inasmuch then   as the children
have partaken of
flesh and blood,
[Jesus] He Himself likewise
shared in the same,   that
through death
He might destroy him
who had the power of death,
that is,   the devil ...
Heb. 2:14

7.   Hebrews 2:14
I t   a t c
h p o
f a b,
H H l
s i t s, t
t d
H m d h
w h t p o d,
t i, t d ...
Addr._____

8.   1 Corinthians 15:21
For since by man [Adam]
came death,
by Man [Jesus]
also came
the resurrection of the dead.
1 Cor. 15:21

8.   1 Corinthians 15:21
F s b m
c d,
b M
a c
t r o t d.
Addr._____

9.   John 1:4
In Him was life,   and
the life was
the light of men.
Jn. 1:4

9.   John 1:4
I H w l, a
t l w
t l o m.
Addr._____

10.   Colossians 2:9
For in Him dwells
all the fullness
of the Godhead   bodily;
Col. 2:9

10.   Colossians 2:9
F i H d
a t f
o t G b;
Addr._____

11.   John 14:6
Jesus said, ... I am
the way,
the truth,   and
the life.
No one comes to the Father
except through Me.
Jn. 14:6

11.   John 14:6
J s, ... I a
t w,
t t,   a
t l.
N c t t F
e t M.
Addr.____

12.   John 12:46; Luke 2:32
I have come as a light
into the world,   that
whoever believes in Me
should not abide in darkness. Luke 2:32
A light to bring revelation
to the Gentiles,   And
the glory of ... Israel.
Jn. 12:46; Lk. 2:32

12.   John 12:46; Luke 2:32
I h c a a l
i t w,   t
w b i M
s n a i d.
A l t b r
t t G,   A
t g o ... I.
Addr.____

13.   Acts 26:18
to open their eyes,
in order to turn them
from darkness to light,   and
from the power of Satan
to God,   that
they may receive
forgiveness of sins   and
an inheritance among those who are
sanctified by faith in Me.
Acts 26:18

13.   Acts 26:18
t o t e,
i o t t t
f d t l,   a
f t p o S
t G,   t
t m r
f o s   a
a i a t w a
s b f i M.
Addr.____

14.   Romans 1:20a
For since the creation
of the world
His invisible attributes
are clearly seen,
being understood by the things   that
are made,
even His eternal power   and Godhead ...
Rom. 1:20a

14.   Romans 1:20a
F s t c
o t w
H i a
a c s,
b u b t t   t
a m,
e H e p   a G ...
Addr.____

15.   John 9:4
[Jesus said] I must work
the works of Him
who sent Me
while it is day;
the night is coming
when no one can work.
Jn. 9:4

15.   John 9:4
I m w
t w o H
w s M
w i i d;
t n i c
w n o c w.
Addr._____

16.   Luke 1:78,79
Through the tender mercy
of our God,
With which the Dayspring
from on high
has visited us;
To give light to those
who sit in darkness   and
the shadow of death,
To guide our feet
into the way of peace.
Lk. 1:78,79

16.   Luke 1:78,79
T t t m
o o G,
W w t D
f o h
h v u;
T g l t t
w s i d a
t s o d,
T g o f
i t w o p.
Addr._____

17.   John 16:33a
These things
I have spoken to you,   that
in Me [Jesus]
you may have peace.
Jn. 16:33a

17.   John 16:33a
T t
I h s t y, t
i M
y m h p.
Addr._____

18.   2 Peter 1:19
And so we have
the prophetic word confirmed,
which you do well to heed
as a light   that
shines in a dark place,
until the day dawns   and
the morning star rises
in your hearts;
2 Pet. 1:19

18.   2 Peter 1:19
A s w h
t p w c,
w y d w t h
a a l   t
s i a d p,
u t d d a
t m s r
i y h;
Addr._____

DAY 1:   KNOWING HIM

19.   Revelation 22:16
I, Jesus, ...
I am the Root   and
the Offspring of David,
the Bright   and Morning Star.
Rev. 22:16

19.   Revelation 22:16
I, J, ...
I a t R   a
t O o D,
t B   a M S.
Addr._____

20.   Matthew 4:16
The people
who sat in darkness
have seen a great light,   And
upon those who sat
in the region   and
shadow of death
Light has dawned.
Mt. 4:16

20.   Matthew 4:16
T p
w s i d
h s a g l, A
u t w s
i t r   a
s o d
L h d.
Addr._____

21.   Matthew 4:17
From that time Jesus began
to preach and to say,
Repent,
for the kingdom of heaven
is at hand.
Mt. 4:17

21.   Matthew 4:17
F t t J b
t p a t s,
R,
f t k o h
i a h.
Addr._____

22.   Genesis 1:4
And God saw   the light,   that
it was good;   and
God divided the light
from the darkness.
Gen. 1:4

22.   Genesis 1:4
A G s t l, t
i w g; a
G d t l
f t d.
Addr._____

23.   Genesis 1:5
God called the light Day,   and
the darkness He called Night.
So the evening   and
the morning
were the first day.
Gen. 1:5

23.   Genesis 1:5
G c t l D, a
t d H c N.
S t e   a
t m
w t f d.
Addr._____

DAY TWO: ANALOGY SYNOPSIS

On Creation Day Two,
God's work in Creation was to create firmament –
the air or expanse between heaven and earth.

This reminds me of the crucifixion of Jesus. He was
nailed to the cross and lifted up from the earth. His
death occurred in the air between heaven and earth.

ANALOGY: CREATION DAY TWO

Analogy: a partial likeness between two things that are compared. This analogy seeks to view the Scriptures about Jesus and the church through the narrative of Genesis Chapter One.

Creation Day 2:   Genesis 1:6-8

6 Then God said, "Let there be a firmament in the midst of the waters, and let it divide the waters from the waters." 7 Thus God made the firmament, and divided the waters which were under the firmament from the waters which were above the firmament; and it was so. 8 And God called the firmament Heaven. So the evening and the morning were the second day.

God's Work in Creation: God created firmament or expanse/space/air.

Jesus' Work on Earth: Crucifixion: God's penalty of death for sin is paid.

Bible Verse Keywords: Firmament; the firmament Heaven; prince of the power of the air; spiritual hosts of wickedness in heavenly places; the devil has come down; serpent; devil; death; (Note: Although Satan is prince of the power of the air, Jesus is King and Lord of all.) Crucify Him; Crucify Him. *Please note the horrific details of the words said, and the deeds done to Jesus prior to His murder.* If you confess with your mouth the Lord Jesus and believe in ... .

Pondered: 1. "That it was good" is not included in Creation Day Two – the shortest of all the Creation accounts. This curious fact energized my quest of looking for Jesus in Creation. See "The Quest" on page 9.

2. The Bible states in Ephesians 2:2: "the prince of the power of the air" is Satan. The air is the expanse above the surface of the earth. Reference Job 1:6,7: "Now there was a day when the sons of God came to present themselves before the LORD, and Satan also came among them. And the LORD said to Satan, 'From where do you come?' So Satan answered the LORD and said, 'From going to and fro on the earth ... .'" Satan is the prince of the power of the air. See "How to be Saved" on page 129.

3. Jesus was crucified in the air. He was lifted up on the cross and hung there until He died. God, His Father, laid His judgement of sin on His Son.

4. The innocent Son chose to do His Father's will. He bore all the sins of the entire world upon His sinless Self before His Holy Father. Jesus said, "Now is the judgment of this world; now the ruler of this world will be cast out. And I, if I am lifted up from the earth, will draw all peoples to Myself"– John12:31,32. Jesus' work on the cross conquered Satan's power.

5. Jesus was reviled, mocked, spat upon, and tortured by the very humans He created. Then came His anguished separation from His Holy Father.

6. Could it be that Day Two – the shortest account of Creation, in some respect, relates to the inclination for that torturous day to end quickly?

1.   Genesis 1:6-8a
Then God said,
Let there be a firmament
     in the midst of the waters,   and
     let it divide the waters
     from the waters.
Thus God made the firmament,   and
     divided the waters
     which were under the firmament
     from the waters
     which were above the firmament; and
     it was so.   And
God called the firmament Heaven.
Gen. 1:6-8a

1.   Genesis 1:6-8a
T G s,
L t b a f
     i t m o t w, a
     l i d t w
     f t w.
T G m t f,   a
     d t w
     w w u t f
     f t w
     w w a t f;   a
     i w s.   A
G c t f H.
Addr._____

2.   Ephesians 2:2b; 6:12
according to the prince
of the power of the air [Satan],
the spirit who now works ...   Ephesians 6:12
For we do not wrestle
against flesh and blood,   but
against principalities,
against powers,
against the rulers of the darkness
          of this age,
against spiritual hosts of wickedness
          in the heavenly places.
Eph. 2:2b; 6:12

2.   Ephesians 2:2b; 6:12
a t t p
o t p o t a,
t s w n w ...
F w d n w
a f a b, b
a p,
a p,
a t r o t d
     o t a,
a s h o w
     i t h p.
Addr._____

3.   Revelation 12:12b; 2 Cor. 11:3b
Woe to the inhabitants
of the earth   and the sea!
For the devil
has come down to you,
having great wrath,
because he knows   that
he has a short time ...   2 Corinthians 11:3b
the serpent [who] deceived Eve
by his craftiness ...
Rev. 12:12b; 2 Cor. 11:3b

3.   Revelation 12:12b; 2 Cor. 11:3b
W t t i
o t e   a t s!
F t d
h c d t y,
h g w,
b h k   t
h h a s t ...
t s d E
b h c ...
Addr._____

DAY 2:   SAVING FAITH

SALVATION SCRIPTURES

4.   Revelation 12:9b; Ephesians 5:6b
That serpent of old,
called the Devil and Satan,
who deceives the whole world; Ephesians 5:6b
because of these things
the wrath of God comes
upon the sons of disobedience.
Rev. 12:9b; Eph. 5:6b

4.   Revelation 12:9b; Ephesians 5:6b
T s o o,
c t D a S,
w d t w w;
b o t t
t w o G c
u t s o d.
Addr._____

5.   Romans 1:29-32a
being filled with all unrighteousness,
sexual immorality, wickedness,
covetousness, maliciousness;
full of envy, murder, strife,
deceit, evil-mindedness;
they are whisperers, backbiters,
haters of God,
violent, proud, boasters,
inventors of evil things,
disobedient to parents,
undiscerning, untrustworthy,
unloving, unforgiving, unmerciful;
who, knowing
the righteous judgment of God,   that
those who practice such things
are deserving of death,
Rom. 1:29-32a

5.   Romans 1:29-32a
b f w a u,
s i, w,
c, m;
f o e, m, s,
d, e-m;
t a w, b,
h o G,
v, p, b,
i o e t,
d t p,
ud, ut,
ul, uf, um;
w, k
t r j o G, t
t w p s t
a d o d,
Addr._____

6.   Romans 6:23a
For the wages of sin
is death ...
Rom. 6:23a

6.   Romans 6:23a
F t w o s
i d ...
Addr._____

7.   Romans 3:10,11
As it is written:
There is none   righteous,
no, not one;
There is none   who understands;
There is none   who seeks after God.
Rom. 3:10,11

7.   Romans 3:10,11
A i i w:
T i n   r,
n, n o;
T i n   w u;
T i n   w s a G.
Addr._____

DAY 2: SAVING FAITH

8. 1 John 5:19b
The whole world lies
under the sway
of the wicked one.
1 Jn. 5:19b

9. Genesis 3:15
[God said to the serpent] And I will put enmity
Between you   and the woman,   And
between your seed   and her Seed;
He [Jesus] shall bruise your head,   And
you [serpent/Satan] shall bruise His heel.
Gen. 3:15

10. 1 John 3:8b
For this purpose
the Son of God   was manifested,   that
He might destroy   the works of the devil.
1 Jn. 3:8b

11. John 3:19
And this is the condemnation,   that
the light has come   into the world,   and
men loved darkness rather than light,
because their deeds were evil.
Jn. 3:19

12. 1 John 2:2
[Jesus] He Himself is the propitiation
for our sins,   and
not for ours only   but also
for the whole world.
1 Jn. 2:2

13. Galatians 3:13
Christ ... having become
a curse for us
(for it is written,   Cursed is everyone
who hangs on a tree.)
Gal. 3:13

SALVATION SCRIPTURES

8. 1 John 5:19b
T w w l
u t s
o t w o.
Addr._____

9. Genesis 3:15
A I w p e
B y   a t w, A
b y s   a h S;
H s b y h,   A
y s b H h.
Addr._____

10. 1 John 3:8b
F t p
t S o G w m,   t
H m d   t w o t d.
Addr._____

11. John 3:19
A t i t c,   t
t l h c i t w, a
m l d r t l,
b t d w e.
Addr._____

12. 1 John 2:2
H H i t p
f o s,   a
n f o o b a
f t w w.
Addr._____

13. Galatians 3:13
C ... h b
a c f u
(f i i w, C i e
w h o a t.)
Addr._____

14.   John 12:32,33
[Jesus said] And I, if I am lifted up
from the earth
will draw all peoples to Myself.
This He said, signifying
by what death He would die.
Jn. 12:32,33

14.   John 12:32,33
A I, i I a l u
f t e
w d a p t M.
T H s, s
b w d H w d.
Addr._____

15.   Luke 22:3a,4
Then Satan entered Judas ...
So he went his way   and
conferred with the chief priests   and
captains, how he might betray
Him [Jesus] to them.
Lk. 22:3a,4

15.   Luke 22:3a,4
T S e J ...
S h w h w   a
c w t c p   a
c, h h m b
H t t.
Addr._____

16.   John 12:27
[Jesus said] Now My soul is troubled,   and
what shall I say?
Father, save Me from this hour?   But
for this purpose
I came to this hour.
Jn. 12:27

16.   John 12:27
N M s i t,   a
w s I s?
F, s M f t h?   B
f t p
I c t t h.
Addr._____

17.   Mark 14:32a,33b,34a-36
They came to ... Gethsemane ...   and
[Jesus] He began to be troubled   and
deeply distressed ...
My soul is exceedingly sorrowful,
even to death.
He went a little farther,   and
fell on the ground,   and
prayed that if it were possible,
the hour might pass from Him.   And
He said, Abba, Father,
all things are possible for You.
Take this cup away from Me;
nevertheless, not what I will,   but
what You will.
Mk. 14:32a,33b,34a-36

17.   Mark 14:32a,33b,34a-36
T c t ... G ... a
H b t b t   a
d d ...
M s i e s,
e t d.
H w a l f,   a
f o t g,   a
p t i i w p,
t h m p f H.   A
H s, A, F,
a t a p f Y.
T t c a f M;
n, n w I w,   b
w Y w.
Addr._____

18.   Mark 14:41b,42b
[Jesus said] The hour has come;
behold, the Son of Man
is being betrayed
into the hands of sinners ...
See, My betrayer [Judas] is at hand.
Mk.14:41b,42b

18.   Mark 14:41b,42b
T h h c;
b, t S o M
i b b
i t h o s ...
S, M b i a h.
Addr._____

19.   Mark 14:53a,55,56
And they led Jesus away ...
to the high priest ...
Now the chief priests   and
all the council sought testimony
against Jesus
to put Him to death,   but
found none.
For many bore false witness
against Him,   but
their testimonies did not agree.
Mk. 14:53a,55,56

19.   Mark 14:53a,55,56
A t l J a ...
t t h p ...
N t c p   a
a t c s t
a J
t p H t d,   b
f n.
F m b f w
a H,   b
t t d n a.
Addr._____

20.   Luke 22:66,67,70,71
As soon as it was day,
the elders of the people,
both chief priests   and
scribes, came together   and
led Him into their council, saying,
If You are the Christ, tell us. But
[Jesus] He said to them,   If I tell you,
you will by no means believe.
Then they all said,
Are You then the Son of God?
So He said to them,
You rightly say   that I am.   And
they said, What further testimony
do we need?
For we have heard it ourselves
from His own mouth.
Lk. 22:66,67,70,71

20.   Luke 22:66,67,70,71
A s a i w d,
t e o t p,
b c p   a
s, c t   a
l H i t c, s,
I Y a t C, t u. B
H s t t,   I I t y,
y w b n m b.
T t a s,
A Y t t S o G?
S H s t t,
Y r s   t I a.   A
t s, W f t
d w n?
F w h h i o
f H o m.
Addr._____

SALVATION SCRIPTURES

21.   Mark 14:64b,65; 15:1b
And they all condemned Him
to be deserving of death.
Then some began to spit
on Him,   and
to blindfold Him,   and
to beat Him,   and
to say to Him, Prophesy!   And
the officers struck Him
with the palms of their hands ... Mark 15:1b
they bound Jesus,
led Him away,   and
delivered Him to Pilate.
Mk. 14:64b,65; 15:1b

21.   Mark 14:64b,65; 15:1b
A t a c H
t b d o d.
T s b t s
o H,   a
t b H,   a
t b H,   a
t s t H, P!   A
t o s H
w t p o t h ...
t b J,
l H a,   a
d H t P.
Addr.____

22.   John 18:37b
Are You a king then? [Pilate asked]
Jesus answered, You say rightly   that
I am a king.
For this cause   I was born,   and
for this cause   I have come
into the world,   that
I should bear witness
to the truth.
Jn. 18:37b

22.   John 18:37b
A Y a k t?
J a, Y s r   t
I a a k.
F t c   I w b, a
f t c   I h c
i t w,   t
I s b w
t t t.
Addr.____

23.   Mark 15:10,12b-14
... [Pilate] he knew   that
the chief priests [had] handed Him over
because of envy.
What ... do you want me to do
with Him whom you call
the King of the Jews?
So they cried out again,
Crucify Him!
Then Pilate said to them,
Why, what evil has He done? But
they cried out all the more,
Crucify Him!
Mk. 15:10,12b-14

23.   Mark 15:10,12b-14
... h k   t
t c p h H o
b o e.
W ... d y w m t d
w H w y c
t K o t J?
S t c o a,
C H!
T P s t t,
W, w e h H d? B
t c o a t m,
C H!
Addr.____

DAY 2:   SAVING FAITH

SALVATION SCRIPTURES

24.   Matthew 27:26b-31
When he [Pilate] had scourged Jesus,
he delivered Him
to be crucified.
Then the soldiers of the governor ...
gathered the whole garrison
around Him.   And
they stripped Him   and
put a scarlet robe on Him.
When they had twisted
a crown of thorns,
they put it on His head,   and
a reed in His right hand.   And
they bowed the knee before Him   and
mocked Him, saying,
Hail, King of the Jews!
Then they spat on Him,   and
took the reed   and struck Him
on the head.   And
when they had mocked Him,
they took the robe off Him,
put His own clothes on Him,   and
led Him away   to be crucified.
Mt. 27:26b-31

24.   Matthew 27:26b-31
W h h s J,
h d H
t b c.
T t s o t g ...
g t w g
a H.   A
t s H   a
p a s r o H.
W t h t
a c o t,
t p i o H h,   a
a r i H r h.   A
t b t k b H   a
m H, s,
H, K o t J!
T t s o H,   a
t t r   a s H
o t h.   A
w t h m H,
t t t r o H,
p H o c o H,   a
l H a t b c.
Addr._____

25.   John 19:17
And He, bearing His cross,
went out to a place called
the Place of a Skull,
which is called in Hebrew, Golgotha,
Jn. 19:17

25.   John 19:17
A H, b H c,
w o t a p c
t P o a S,
w i c i H, G,
Addr._____

26.   Mark 15:31a,32b
Likewise the chief priests also,
mocking among themselves
with the scribes ...
Even those who were crucified
with Him
reviled Him.
Mk. 15:31a,32b

26.   Mark 15:31a,32b
L t c p a,
m a t
w t s ...
E t w w c
w H
r H.
Addr._____

27.   Luke 23:34,35a
... Jesus said,
Father, forgive them,
for they do not know
what they do.   And
they divided His garments   and
cast lots.   And
the people stood looking on.
Lk. 23:34,35a

27.   Luke 23:34,35a
... J s,
F, f t,
f t d n k
w t d.   A
t d H g   a
c l.   A
t p s l o.
Addr._____

28.   Luke 23:44,45a
Now it was about the sixth hour,   and
there was darkness
over all the earth
until the ninth hour.
... the sun was darkened ...
Lk. 23:44,45a

28.   Luke 23:44,45a
N i w a t s h,   a
t w d
o a t e
u t n h.
... t s w d ...
Addr._____

29.   Matthew 27:46
And about the ninth hour
Jesus cried out with a loud voice,
saying, Eli, Eli, lama sabachthani?   that is,
My God, My God,
why have You forsaken Me?
Mt. 27:46

29.   Matthew 27:46
A a t n h
J c o w a l v,
s, E, E, l s?   t i,
M G, M G,
w h Y f M?
Addr._____

30.   Luke 23:46
And when Jesus had cried out
with a loud voice,
He said, Father, into Your hands
I commit My spirit.
Having said this,
He breathed His last.
Lk. 23:46

30.   Luke 23:46
A w J h c o
w a l v,
H s, F, i Y h
I c M s.
H s t,
H b H l.
Addr._____

31.   Mark15:38
Then the veil of the temple
was torn in two
from top to bottom.
Mk. 15:38

31.   Mark15:38
T t v o t t
w t i t
f t t b.
Addr._____

32.   Genesis 1:8b
So the evening   and the morning
were the second day.
Gen. 1:8b

32.   Genesis 1:8b
S t e a t m
w t s d.
Addr._____

33.   Romans 10:8,9
But what does it say?
The word is near you,
in your mouth   and
in your heart   (that is,
the word of faith ...):   that
if you confess with   your mouth
the Lord Jesus   and
believe in your heart   that
God has raised Him
from the dead,
you will be saved.
Rom. 10:8,9

33.   Romans 10:8,9
B w d i s?
T w i n y,
i y m   a
i y h   (t i,
t w o f ...): t
i y c w   y m
t L J   a
b i y h   t
G h r H
f t d,
y w b s.
Addr._____

34.   Matthew 12:40
For as Jonah   was three days   and
three nights   in the belly of the great fish,
so will the   Son of Man be three days   and
three nights   in the heart of the earth.
Mt. 12:40

34.   Matthew 12:40
F a J   w t d   a
t n   i t b o t g f,
s w t   S o M b t d a
t n   i t h o t e.
Addr._____

35.   Romans 10:17
So then faith comes
by hearing,   and hearing
by the word of God.
Rom. 10:17

35.   Romans 10:17
S t f c
b h, a h
b t w o G.
Addr._____

36.   Hebrews 11:6
But without faith
it is impossible to please Him,
for he who comes to God
must believe that He is,   and that
He is a rewarder of those
who diligently seek Him.
Heb. 11:6

36.   Hebrews 11:6
B w f
i i i t p H,
f h w c t G
m b t H i, a t
H i a r o t
w d s H.
Addr._____

DAY THREE: ANALOGY SYNOPSIS

On Creation Day Three,
God's work in Creation was to create dry land called
Earth and the first living organisms – plant life.

This reminds me of the burial of Jesus in the earth. The
third day, He is the firstfruit living – resurrected life.

ANALOGY: CREATION DAY THREE

Analogy: a partial likeness between two things that are compared. This analogy seeks to view the Scriptures about Jesus and the church through the narrative of Genesis Chapter One.

Creation Day 3: Genesis 1:9-12

9 Then God said, "Let the waters under the heavens be gathered together into one place, and let the dry land appear"; and it was so. 10 And God called the dry land Earth, and the gathering together of the waters He called Seas. And God saw that it was good. 11 Then God said, "Let the earth bring forth grass, the herb that yields seed, and the fruit tree that yields fruit according to its kind, whose seed is in itself, on the earth"; and it was so. 12 And the earth brought forth grass, the herb that yields seed according to its kind, and the tree that yields fruit, whose seed is in itself according to its kind. And God saw that it was good. 13 So the evening and the morning were the third day.

God's Work in Creation: Dry land called Earth, Seas, and vegetation are created on the third day.

Jesus' Work on Earth: Burial and Resurrection: Dry land Earth and vegetation are essential to Jesus' burial. He is buried in the earth, and He is risen on the third day.

Bible Verse Keywords: Dry land Earth; herb; seed; fruit tree; fruit according to its kind; seed is in itself; third day; myrrh; aloes; linen; spices; bury; garden; tomb hewn out of the rock; buried; third day; firstfruits; made alive; resurrection and the life; shall live; fruit of His body; your fruit to holiness; eternal life.

Pondered: 1. The body of Jesus is prepared for burial with a variety of vegetation: a mixture of myrrh (a gum resin from small, spiny trees) and aloes (plant leaves with a bitter juice); and His body is bound with strips of linen (cloth from flax plants) with spices (aromatic substances from plants).

2. The body of Jesus is placed in a new tomb hewn out of the rock (the hard part of the earth's crust). The tomb is in a garden (a place of cultivated vegetation). Thus Jesus was laid in a garden, in a tomb, in the Earth.

3. God particularly notes "the fruit tree that yields fruit ... whose seed is in itself." 1 Corinthians 15:20a says, "But now Christ is risen from the dead, and become the firstfruits" of those who died trusting in Him. James 1:18 states, "Of His own will [Jesus Christ] He brought us forth by the word of truth, that we might be a kind of firstfruits of His creatures."

4. On the third day, the first living organisms of plant life are created. On the third day, the firstfruit living the eternally resurrected life is Jesus.

5. "And God saw that it was good," is declared twice. It is first said for dry land and Seas, and again after the creation of plants – the first earth life.

6. Could be that "good" declared twice brings to mind the Father's joy of: first seeing His Son's body off the cross and buried in the earth, and again after seeing His Son alive – the first resurrected life?

1.   Genesis 1:9,10
Then God said,
Let the waters
under the heavens
be gathered together into one place,   and
let the dry land appear;   and
it was so.   And
God called the dry land Earth,   and
the gathering together of the waters
He called Seas.   And
God saw that it was good.
Gen. 1:9,10

1.   Genesis 1:9,10
T G s,
L t w
u t h
b g t i o p,   a
l t d l a;   a
i w s.   A
G c t d l E,   a
t g t o t w
H c S.   A
G s t i w g.
Addr._____

2.   Genesis 1:11
Then God said,
Let the earth bring forth grass,
the herb   that yields seed,   and
the fruit tree   that
yields fruit
according to its kind,
whose seed is in itself,
on the earth;   and
it was so.
Gen. 1:11

2.   Genesis 1:11
T G s,
L t e b f g,
t h   t y s, a
t f t   t
y f
a t i k,
w s i i i,
o t e;   a
i w s.
Addr._____

3.   John 19:38a-40
... Joseph of Arimathea ...
took the body of Jesus.   And
Nicodemus ... also came,
bringing a mixture of
myrrh and aloes,
about a hundred pounds.
Then they took
the body of Jesus,   and
bound **it** in strips of linen
with the spices,
as the custom of the Jews
is to bury.
Jn. 19:38a-40

3.   John 19:38a-40
... J o A ...
t t b o J.   A
N ... a c,
b a m o
m a a,
a a h p.
T t t
t b o J,   a
b i i s o l
w t s,
a t c o t J
i t b.
Addr._____

4.   John 19:41,42; Matthew 27:60b

Now in the place
where He was crucified
there was a garden, and
in the garden
a new tomb ...   Matthew 27:60b
hewn out of the rock ...   John 19:41b,42
in which no one
had yet been laid.
So there they laid Jesus,
because of the Jews' Preparation Day,
for the tomb was nearby.
Jn. 19:41,42; Mt. 27:60b

4.   John 19:41,42; Matthew 27:60b

N i t p
w H w c
t w a g, a
i t g
a n t ...
h o o t r ...
i w n o
h y b l.
S t t l J,
b o t J' P D,
f t t w n.
Addr.____

5.   1 Corinthians 15:1,2a-4

Moreover, brethren,
I declare to you the gospel
which I preached to you,
which also you received   and
in which you stand,
by which also you are saved ... that
Christ died for our sins
according to the Scriptures,   and that
He was buried,   and that
He rose again the third day
according to the Scriptures,
1 Cor. 15:1,2a-4

5.   1 Corinthians 15:1,2a-4

M, b,
I d t y t g
w I p t y,
w a y r   a
i w y s,
b w a y a s ... t
C d f o s
a t t S,   a t
H w b,   a t
H r a t t d
a t t S,
Addr.____

6.   Matthew 28:1a,5b,6a

Now after the Sabbath,
as the first day of the week
began to dawn ...
the angel ... said to the women ...
I know   that
you seek Jesus
who was crucified.
He is not here;
for He is risen,
as He said.
Mt. 28:1a,5b,6a

6.   Matthew 28:1a,5b,6a

N a t S,
a t f d o t w
b t d ...
t a ... s t t w ...
I k   t
y s J
w w c.
H i n h;
f H i r,
a H s.
Addr.____

7.   Genesis 1:12a
And the earth brought forth grass,
the herb that yields seed
according to its kind,   and
the tree   that
yields fruit,
whose seed is in itself
according to its kind.
Gen. 1:12a

7.   Genesis 1:12a
A t e b f g,
t h t y s
a t i k, a
t t   t
y f,
w s i i i
a t i k.
Addr.____

8.   1 Corinthians 15:20,21
... Christ is risen from the dead,   and
has become the firstfruits
of those who have fallen asleep.
For since by man [Adam]
came death,
by Man [Christ] also came
the resurrection of the dead.
1 Cor. 15:20,21

8.   1 Corinthians 15:20,21
... C i r f t d,   a
h b t f
o t w h f a.
F s b m
c d,
b M a c
t r o t d.
Addr.____

9.   1 Corinthians 15:22,23
For as in Adam all die,
even so in Christ
all shall be made alive.   But
each one in his own order:
Christ the firstfruits,
afterward
those who are Christ's
at His coming.
1 Cor. 15:22,23

9.   1 Corinthians 15:22,23
F a i A a d,
e s i C
a s b m a.   B
e o i h o o:
C t f,
a
t w a C's
a H c.
Addr.____

10.   John 11:25
Jesus said ... I am
the resurrection   and
the life.
He who believes in Me,
though he may die,
he shall live.
Jn. 11:25

10.   John 11:25
J s ... I a
t r   a
t l.
H w b i M,
t h m d,
h s l.
Addr.____

11.   Acts 2:30,31
Therefore, being a prophet [King David],   and
knowing   that God had sworn
with an oath to him   that
of the fruit of his [King David's] body,
according to the flesh,
He [God] would raise up
the Christ
to sit on his [King David's] throne,
he, foreseeing this,
spoke concerning
the resurrection of the Christ,   that
[Jesus'] His soul was not left in Hades,   nor
did His flesh see corruption.
Acts 2:30,31

11.   Acts 2:30,31
T, b a p,   a
k   t G h s
w a o t h   t
o t f o h b,
a t t f,
H w r u
t C
t s o h t,
h, f t,
s c
t r o t C,   t
H s w n l i H,   n
d H f s c.
Addr._____

12.   Acts 13:37,38
... He **whom** God raised up
saw no corruption.
Therefore let it be known to you,
brethren,   that
through this Man [Jesus]
is preached to you
the forgiveness of sins;
Acts 13:37,38

12.   Acts 13:37,38
... H w G r u
s n c.
T l i b k t y,
b,   t
t t M
i p t y
t f o s;
Addr._____

13.   Romans 6:22,23
But now
having been set free from sin,   and
having become slaves of God,
you have your fruit
to holiness,   and
the end,
everlasting life.
For the wages of sin
is death,   but
the gift of God
is eternal life
in Christ Jesus our Lord.
Rom. 6:22,23

13.   Romans 6:22,23
B n
h b s f f s,   a
h b s o G,
y h y f
t h,   a
t e,
e l.
F t w o s
i d,   b
t g o G
i e l
i C J o L.
Addr._____

14.   Ephesians 2:4,5a,8,9
... God, **who** is rich in mercy,
because of His great love
with which He loved us,
even when we were
dead in trespasses,
made us alive together with Christ ...
For by grace
you have been saved
through faith,   and that
not of yourselves;
it is the gift of God,
not of works,
lest anyone should boast.
Eph. 2:4,5a,8,9

15.   1 John 2:1; 1:9
My little children,   these things I write to you,
so that you may not sin.   And
if anyone sins,
we have an Advocate with the Father,
Jesus Christ the righteous. 1 John 1:9
If we confess our sins,
He is faithful   and just
to forgive us our sins   and
to cleanse us from all unrighteousness.
1 Jn. 2:1; 1:9

16.   Psalm 15:1b,2
Who may dwell in Your holy hill?
He who walks uprightly,   And
works righteousness,   And
speaks the truth in his heart;
Ps. 15:1b,2

17.   Genesis 1:12b,13
And God saw that it was good.
So the evening   and the morning
were the third day.
Gen. 1:12b,13

14.   Ephesians 2:4,5a,8,9
... G, **w i r i m,**
b o H g l
w w H l u,
e w w w
d i t,
m u a t w C ...
F b g
y h b s
t f,   a t
n o y;
i i t g o G,
n o w,
l a s b.
Addr._____

15.   1 John 2:1; 1:9
M l c,   t t I w t y,
s t y m n s.   A
i a s,
w h a A w t F,
J C t r.
I w c o s,
H i f   a j
t f u o s   a
t c u f a u.
Addr._____

16.   Psalm 15:1b,2
W m d i Y h h?
H w w u,   A
w r,   A
s t t i h h;
Addr._____

17.   Genesis 1:12b,13
A G s t i w g.
S t e   a t m
w t t d.
Addr._____

DAY FOUR: ANALOGY SYNOPSIS

On Creation Day Four,
God's work in Creation was to make lights. He made two great lights and the stars also. These created lights bring light to the earth imitating the unique light of Creation Day One.

This reminds me of the prophets and the apostles Jesus commissioned to be His witnesses. These created beings bring light to the earth imitating the True Light, Who returned to His Father.

ANALOGY: CREATION DAY FOUR

Analogy: a partial likeness between two things that are compared. This analogy seeks to view the Scriptures about Jesus and the church through the narrative of Genesis Chapter One.

Creation Day 4: Genesis 1:14-19

14 Then God said, "Let there be lights in the firmament of the heavens to divide the day from the night; and let them be for signs and seasons, and for days and years; 15 and let them be for lights in the firmament of the heavens to give light on the earth"; and it was so. 16 Then God made two great lights: the greater light to rule the day, and the lesser light to rule the night. He made the stars also. 17 God set them in the firmament of the heavens to give light on the earth, 18 and to rule over the day and over the night, and to divide the light from the darkness. And God saw that it was good. 19 So the evening and the morning were the fourth day.

God's Work in Creation: God made two great lights, and He made the stars also.

Jesus' Work on Earth: Witnesses: The resurrected Jesus Christ appeared to His apostles. Christ commissioned them to be His witnesses, but they were told to wait for the Holy Spirit. (Pentecost has not come.) Jesus Christ returned to heaven.

Bible Verse Keywords: Lights; day; night; signs; seasons; years; true Light; His witnesses; let your light so shine; tarry; received up in heaven; believe in the light; become sons of the light; all the prophets witness; bear witness of the Light; two great lights; greater light to rule the day; lesser light to rule the night; stars; cloud of witnesses; stars of the heavens; not a greater prophet; least of the apostles; sinners, of whom I am chief; less than the least; His witnesses; our citizenship is in heaven; to give light on the earth.

Pondered: 1. It is the resurrection of Christ that secures the resurrection of believers. 1 Corinthians 15:13,14 states, "If there is no resurrection of the dead, then not even Christ has been raised. And if Christ has not been raised, our preaching is useless and so is your faith." Abraham, King David, all the prophets, and the apostles are some of the "cloud of witnesses" who are sons of His resurrection, sons of the Light, and His lights on earth.

2. God has an order for His church. God states that He appointed to the church – first apostles and second prophets. Of the prophets, Jesus said that John the Baptist was the greatest of all. John came as the testifying witness of the Light, and said that Jesus must increase and I must decrease. Jesus declares that whoever is least in the kingdom of God is greater than John the Baptist. Apostle Paul identifies himself as "less than the least."

3. God first appointed apostles to the church. Of the twelve apostles, it is difficult to think of a more humble and influential apostle than Apostle Paul. He is the "foremost interpreter of Christ through all the ages."MSB NAS

4. Could it be that on Creation Day Four those "made lights" that God set in the firmament are His witnesses on earth – citizens of heaven and His lights on the earth?

1.   Genesis 1:14
Then God said,   Let there be lights
in the firmament of the heavens
to divide the day from the night;   and
let them be for sign   and
seasons,   and for days   and years.
Gen. 1:14

1.   Genesis 1:14
T G s,   L t b l
i t f o t h
t d t d f t n;   a
l t b f s   a
s,   a f d   a y.
Addr.____

2.   1 Peter 1:20a; John 1:9a; Acts 13:30
[Jesus] He indeed was foreordained
before the foundation of the world,   but
was manifest in these last times ... John 1:9a
That was the true Light ...   Acts 13:30
... God raised Him from the dead.
1 Pet. 1:20a; Jn. 1:9a; Acts 13:30

2.   1 Peter 1:20a; John 1:9a; Acts 13:30
H i w f
b t f o t w,   b
w m i t l t ...
T w t t L ...
... G r H f t d.
Addr.____

3.   Acts 1:3b
[Jesus] He also presented Himself
alive after His suffering
by many infallible proofs,
being seen by them
during forty days   and
speaking of the things pertaining
to the kingdom of God.
Acts 1:3b

3.   Acts 1:3b
H a p H
a a H s
b m i p,
b s b t
d f d   a
s o t t p
t t k o G.
Addr.____

4.   Acts 13:31
He was seen for many days
by those who came up with Him
from Galilee to Jerusalem,
who are His witnesses to the people.
Acts 13:31

4.   Acts 13:31
H w s f m d
b t w c u w H
f G t J,
w a H w t t p.
Addr.____

5.   Luke 24:36b
Jesus Himself stood
in the midst of them,   and
said to them,
Peace to you.
Lk. 24:36b

5.   Luke 24:36b
J H s
i t m o t,   a
s t t,
P t y.
Addr.____

6.   Luke 24:39,45

[Jesus said] Behold My hands   and
My feet,   that
it is I Myself.
Handle Me   and see,
for a spirit does not have
flesh   and bones
as you see I have.   And
He opened their understanding,   that
they might comprehend
the Scriptures.
Lk. 24:39,45

6.   Luke 24:39,45

B M h   a
M f,   t
i i I M.
H M   a s,
f a s d n h
f   a b
a y s I h. A
H o t u,   t
t m c
t S.
Addr.____

7.   John 15:27

And you [apostles] also
will bear witness,
because you have been with Me
from the beginning.
Jn. 15:27

7.   John 15:27

A y a
w b w,
b y h b w M
f t b.
Addr.____

8.   Matthew 5:16

[Jesus said] Let your light so shine
before men,   that
they may see your good works   and
glorify your Father in heaven.
Mt. 5:16

8.   Matthew 5:16

L y l s s
b m,   t
t m s y g w   a
g y F i h.
Addr.____

9.   Luke 24:49b; Mark 16:19

[Jesus said] but tarry in ... Jerusalem
until you are endued
with power from on high.   Mark 16:19
So then,
after the Lord
had spoken to them,

He was received up
into heaven,   and
sat down
at the right hand of God.
Lk. 24:49b; Mk. 16:19

9.   Luke 24:49b; Mark 16:19

b t i ... J
u y a e
w p f o h.
S t,
a t L
h s t t,

H w r u
i h,   a
s d
a t r h o G.
Addr.____

10.   Genesis 1:15
[God said] let them be for lights
in the firmament of the heavens
to give light on the earth;   and
it was so.
Gen. 1:15

10.   Genesis 1:15
l t b f l
i t f o t h
t g l o t e; a
i w s.
Addr._____

11.   John 12:36a
While you have the light [Jesus],
believe in the light,   that
you may become sons of light.
Jn. 12:36a

11.   John 12:36a
W y h t l,
b i t l, t
y m b s o l.
Addr._____

12.   Ecclesiastes 3:1
To everything   there is a season,
A time for every purpose   under heaven:
Eccl. 3:1

12.   Ecclesiastes 3:1
T e   t i a s,
A t f e p u h:
Addr._____

13.   1 Peter 1:20a; Acts 10:43
[Jesus] He indeed was foreordained
before the foundation of the world ... Acts 10:43
To Him all the prophets witness   that,
through His name,
whoever believes in Him
will receive remission of sins ...
1 Pet. 1:20a; Acts 10:43

13.   1 Peter 1:20a; Acts 10:43
H i w f
b t f o t w ...
T H a t p w t,
t H n,
w b i H
w r r o s ...
Addr._____

14.   Hebrews 12:1b; Isaiah 61:1,2a
we are surrounded by   so great a cloud
of witnesses ... [Isaiah prophesied Jesus] Is. 61:1,2a
The Spirit of the Lord GOD   is upon Me
Because the LORD   has anointed Me
To preach good tidings   to the poor;
He has sent Me   to heal the brokenhearted,
To proclaim liberty   to the captives,   And
the opening of the prison   to those
who are bound;
To proclaim the acceptable year
of the LORD,
Heb. 12:1b; Is. 61:1,2a

14.   Hebrews 12:1b; Isaiah 61:1,2a
w a s b   s g a c
o w ...
T S o t L G   i u M
B t L   h a M
T p g t   t t p;
H h s M   t h t b,
T p l   t t c, A
t o o t p   t t
w a b;
T p t a y
o t L,
Addr._____

15.   John 1:23,7,8; 3:30; Daniel 4:3a
[John the Baptist declared] He said: I am
The voice of one crying in the wilderness:
Make straight the way of the LORD,
as the prophet Isaiah said. John 1:7,8
This man [John] came for a witness,
to bear witness of the Light [Jesus],   that
all through him might believe.
He was not that Light,   but
was sent to bear   witness of that Light. John 3:30
He [Jesus] must increase,   but
I [John] must decrease. Dan. 4:3a
How great are His signs ...
Jn. 1:23,7,8; 3:30; Dan. 4:3a

15.   John 1:23,7,8; 3:30; Daniel 4:3a
H s: I a
T v o o c i t w:
M s t w o t L,
a t p I s.
T m c f a w,
t b w o t L, t
a t h m b.
H w n t L,   b
w s t b   w o t L.
H m i,   b
I m d.
H g a H s ...
Addr._____

16.   Genesis 1:16
Then God made   two great lights:
the greater light   to rule the day,   and
the lesser light   to rule the night.
He made the stars also.
Gen. 1:16

16.   Genesis 1:16
T G m t g l:
t g l   t r t d, a
t l l   t r t n.
H m t s a.
Addr._____

17.   Hebrews 12:1b; Genesis 26:4
... so great a cloud of witnesses ... Genesis 26:4
[God said to Abraham] ... I will make
your descendants multiply
as the stars of heaven;
I will give to your descendants
all these lands;   and
in your seed all the nations
of the earth shall be blessed;
Heb. 12:1b; Gen. 26:4

17.   Hebrews 12:1b; Genesis 26:4
... s g a c o w ...
... I w m
y d m
a t s o h;
I w g t y d
a t l; a
i y s a t n
o t e s b b;
Addr._____

18.   Galatians 3:16
Now to Abraham   and his Seed
were the promises made.
[God] He does not say,   And to seeds,
as of many,   but as of one,
And to your Seed,   **who** is Christ.
Gal. 3:16

18.   Galatians 3:16
N t A   a h S
w t p m.
H d n s,   A t s,
a o m,   b a o o,
A t y S,   **w** i C.
Addr._____

19.   1 Corinthians 12:28a
And God appointed these
in the church:

first apostles,
second prophets ...
1 Cor. 12:28a

19.   1 Corinthians 12:28a
A G a t
i t c:

f a,
s p ...
Addr.____

20.   Luke 7:28
[Jesus said] For I say to you,
among those born of women
there is not a greater prophet
than John the Baptist;   but

he who is least
in the kingdom of God
is greater than he.
Lk. 7:28

20.   Luke 7:28
F I s t y,
a t b o w
t i n a g p
t J t B;   b

h w i l
i t k o G
i g t h.
Addr.____

21.   1 Corinthians 15:9,10a
[Paul said] For I am

the least of the apostles,
who am not worthy
to be called an apostle,
because I persecuted
the church of God.   But
by the grace of God
I am what I am,   and
His grace toward me
was not in vain;
1 Cor. 15:9,10a

21.   1 Corinthians 15:9,10a
F I a

t l o t a,
w a n w
t b c a a,
b I p
t c o G.   B
b t g o G
I a w I a, a
H g t m
w n i v;
Addr.____

22.   1 Timothy 1:15b
[Paul said] Christ Jesus
came into the world
to save sinners,

of whom I am chief.
1 Tim. 1:15b

22.   1 Timothy 1:15b
C J
c i t w
t s s,

o w I a c.
Addr.____

23.   Ephesians 3:8
[Paul said] To me, who am

less than the least of   all the saints,
this grace was given,   that
I should preach
among the Gentiles
the unsearchable riches of Christ,
Eph. 3:8

23.   Ephesians 3:8
T m, w a

l t t l o   a t s,
t g w g, t
I s p
a t G
t u r o C,
Addr.____

24.   Acts 10:42
... [Jesus] He commanded us [apostles]
to preach to the people,   and
to testify   that
it is He
who was ordained by God
to be Judge of the living   and
the dead.
Acts 10:42

24.   Acts 10:42
... H c u
t p t t p,   a
t t   t
i i H
w w o b G
t b J o t l   a
t d.
Addr.____

25.   Acts 5:32b; Philippians 3:20
we are His witnesses to these things ... Phil. 3:20
For our citizenship is in heaven,
from which we also eagerly wait for
the Savior, the Lord Jesus Christ,
Acts 5:32b; Phil. 3:20

25.   Acts 5:32b; Philippians 3:20
w a H w t t t ...
F o c i i h,
f w w a e w f
t S, t L J C,
Addr.____

26.   Genesis 1:17-19
God set them
in the firmament of the heavens
to give light on the earth,   and
to rule over the day   and
over the night,   and
to divide the light
from the darkness.   And

26.   Genesis 1:17-19
G s t
i t f o t h
t g l o t e,   a
t r o t d   a
o t n,   a
t d t l
f t d.   A

God saw that it was good.
So the evening   and the morning
were the fourth day.
Gen. 1:17-19

G s t i w g.
S t e   a t m
w t f d.
Addr.____

DAY FIVE: ANALOGY SYNOPSIS

On Creation Day Five,
God's work in Creation was to create a new
kind of life – flesh and blood water creatures,
generally called fish, and afterwards birds that
fly above the earth.

This reminds me of Christ creating a new life
in the flesh and blood apostles – fishers of men,
and afterwards recipients of the Holy Spirit, Who
often is symbolically represented as a dove
flying above the earth.

ANALOGY: CREATION DAY FIVE

Analogy: a partial likeness between two things that are compared. This analogy seeks to view the Scriptures about Jesus and the church through the narrative of Genesis Chapter One.

Creation Day 5: Genesis 1:20-23

20 Then God said, "Let the waters abound with an abundance of living creatures, and let birds fly above the earth across the face of the firmament of the heavens." 21 So God created great sea creatures and every living thing that moves, with which the waters abounded, according to their kind, and every winged bird according to its kind. And God saw that it was good. 22 And God blessed them, saying, "Be fruitful and multiply, and fill the waters in the seas, and let birds multiply on the earth." 23 So the evening and the morning were the fifth day.

God's Work in Creation: Water creatures, generally called fish, and then birds are created.

Jesus' Work on Earth: Great Commission and Pentecost: The apostles submitting to the new command to love others, are in one accord. Thereby the Holy Spirit comes.

Bible Verse Keywords: Waters abounded with an abundance of living creatures; birds fly above; A new commandment; that you love one another; as I have loved you; new creation; make you fishers of men; the Holy Spirit descended ... like a dove; unless one is born again; born of water and Spirit; It is the Spirit who gives life; flesh profits nothing; Go ... make disciples of all nations; filled with the Holy Spirit; the Lord added to the church daily; He who is in you is greater; he who loves God must love; leaving us an example; we are ambassadors for Christ; ministry of reconciliation.

Pondered: 1. All kinds of sea creatures, generally called fish, are created and live in peace. Commissioned by Jesus as fishers of men and living out the new love commandment, the disciples live in peace awaiting the Holy Spirit.

2. God created birds. The dove is often symbolic of the Holy Spirit. At Pentecost the Holy Spirit comes to indwell the disciples with power.

3. On Day Five, God created new living creations – unlike plant life. These are flesh and blood water creatures, and afterwards birds. Jesus gave a new life to the flesh and blood apostles. They were born again, baptized, and afterwards filled with the Holy Spirit. Christ created new living creations of spiritual life – unlike natural life.

4. Some of the water creatures are mammals; their offspring will be born. Thus waters abound with a multitude of fish. After Pentecost Peter, a fisher of men, preaches the gospel and thousands from every nation are born again. Thus waters abounded with a multitude of believers being baptized.

5. Could it be that God's sequence of creating fish, and afterwards birds, mirrors the sequence of commissioning the fishers of men, and afterwards giving them the Holy Spirit (often depicted as a dove)?

1.   Genesis 1:20
Then God said,
Let the waters abound
with an abundance
of living creatures,   and

let birds fly above the earth
across the face of the firmament
of the heavens.
Gen. 1:20

1.   Genesis 1:20
T G s,
L t w a
w a a
o l c,   a

l b f a t e
a t f o t f
o t h.
Addr.____

2.   John 13:34a,35a
[Jesus said] A new commandment
I give to you,   that
you love one another;
as I have loved you ...
By this
all will know   that
you are My disciples.
Jn. 13:34a,35a

2.   John 13:34a,35a
A n c
I g t y,   t
y l o a;
a I h l y ...
B t
a w k   t
y a M d.
Addr.____

3.   2 Corinthians 5:17; Mark 1:17
Therefore, if anyone is in Christ,
he is a new creation;
old things have passed away;
behold, all things have become new. Mark 1:17
... Jesus said to them,
Follow Me,   and
I will make you
become fishers of men.
2 Cor. 5:17; Mk. 1:17

3.   2 Corinthians 5:17; Mark 1:17
T, i a i i C,
h i a n c;
o t h p a;
b, a t h b n.
... J s t t,
F M,   a
I w m y
b f o m.
Addr.____

4.   1 John 5:6
[Jesus] This is He **who** came
by water and blood – Jesus Christ;
not only by water,   but
by water and blood.   And
it is the Spirit   **who** bears witness,
because the Spirit is truth.
1 Jn. 5:6

4.   1 John 5:6
T i H **w** c
b w a b – J C;
n o b w,   b
b w a b.   A
i i t S   **w** b w,
b t S i t.
Addr.____

MATURATION SCRIPTURES

5.   Luke 3:21b,22
Jesus also was baptized ...   And
the Holy Spirit [had] descended

in bodily form   like a dove upon Him,   and
a **voice** came   from heaven
which said,   You are My beloved Son;
in You   I am well pleased.
Lk. 3:21b,22

5.   Luke 3:21b,22
J a w b ...   A
t H S d

i b f   l a d u H,   a
a v c   f h
w s,   Y a M b S;
i Y   I a w p.
Addr.____

6.   John 3:5b; 1 John 5:1a
[Jesus said] unless one is born again,
he cannot see
the kingdom of God. 1 John 5:1a
Whoever believes   that
Jesus is the Christ
is born of God ...
Jn. 3:5b; 1 Jn. 5:1a

6.   John 3:5b; 1 John 5:1a
u o i b a,
h c s
t k o G.
W b   t
J i t C
i b o G ...
Addr.____

7.   John 3:3,5b
Jesus ... said ... Most assuredly,
I say to you,
unless one is born again,
he cannot see
the kingdom of God.
unless one is born of water   and
the Spirit,
he cannot enter
the kingdom of God.
Jn. 3:3,5b

7.   John 3:3,5b
J ... s ... M a,
I s t y,
u o i b a,
h c s
t k o G.
u o i b o w   a
t S,
h c e
t k o G.
Addr.____

8.   John 6:63
It is the Spirit **who** gives life;
the flesh profits
nothing.
The words   that
I speak to you
are spirit,   and
they are life.
Jn. 6:63

8.   John 6:63
I i t S w g l;
t f p
n.
T w   t
I s t y
a s,   a
t a l.
Addr.____

MATURATION SCRIPTURES

9.   Mark 16:15; Matthew 28:18b,19
And [Jesus] He said to them,
Go into all the world   and
preach the gospel
to every creature. Matthew 28:18b,19
All authority has been given   to Me
in heaven   and on earth.
Go therefore   and
make disciples
of all the nations,
baptizing them in the name
of the Father   and
of the Son   and
of the Holy Spirit,
Mk. 16:15; Mt. 28:18b,19

9.   Mark 16:15; Matthew 28:18b,19
A H s t t,
G i a t w   a
p t g
t e c.
A a h b g   t M
i h   a o e.
G t   a
m d
o a t n,
b t i t n
o t F   a
o t S   a
o t H S,
Addr._____

10.   Acts 1:4b,5
He commanded them
not to depart from Jerusalem,   but
to wait for the Promise
of the Father ...
for John truly baptized   with water,   but
you shall be baptized   with the Holy Spirit
not many days from now.
Acts 1:4b,5

10.   Acts 1:4b,5
H c t
n t d f J,   b
t w f t P
o t F ...
f J t b   w w,   b
y s b b   w t H S
n m d f n.
Addr._____

11.   Acts 2:1a,2a,4; 4:31b
When the Day of Pentecost
had fully come, [the disciples]
they were all with one accord ... And
suddenly there came
a sound from heaven,
as of a rushing mighty wind,   And
they were all filled
with the Holy Spirit   and
began to speak with other tongues,
as the Spirit gave them utterance. Acts 4:31b
and they spoke
the word of God with boldness.
Acts 2:1a,2a,4; 4:31b

11.   Acts 2:1a,2a,4; 4:31b
W t D o P
h f c,
t w a w o a ... A
s t c
a s f h,
a o a r m w,   A
t w a f
w t H S   a
b t s w o t,
a t S g t u.
a t s
t w o G w b.
Addr._____

12.   Acts 2:38
Peter said to them [the multitude from every nation],
Repent,   and
let every one of you be baptized
in the name of Jesus Christ
for the remission of sins;   and
you shall receive
the gift
of the Holy Spirit.
Acts 2:38

12.   Acts 2:38
P s t t,
R,   a
l e o o y b b
i t n o J C
f t r o s;   a
y s r
t g
o t H S.
Addr._____

13.   Acts 2:41,47b
Then those who gladly received
his word   were baptized;   and that day
about three thousand souls
were added to them.   And
the Lord added to the church daily
those who were being saved.
Acts 2:41,47b

13.   Acts 2:41,47b
T t w g r
h w   w b;   a t d
a t t s
w a t t.   A
t L a t t c d
t w w b s.
Addr._____

14.   1 John 4:4
You are of God, little children,   and
have overcome them,
because He **who** is in you
is greater
than he who is in the world.
1 Jn. 4:4

14.   1 John 4:4
Y a o G, l c,   a
h o t,
b H **w i i y**
i g
t h w i i t w.
Addr._____

15.   1 Corinthians 2:9,10
But as it is written:
Eye has not seen,   nor ear heard,
Nor have entered   into the heart of man
The things which God
has prepared for those
who love Him.   But
God has revealed them to us
through His Spirit.
For the Spirit searches all things,
yes, the deep things of God.
1 Cor. 2:9,10

15.   1 Corinthians 2:9,10
B a i i w:
E h n s,   n e h,
N h e   i t h o m
T t w G
h p f t
w l H.   B
G h r t t u
t H S.
F t S s a t,
y, t d t o G.
Addr._____

16.   1 John 4:20,21; 2:5
If someone says, I love God,   and
hates his brother,
he is a liar;
for he who does not
love his brother
whom he has seen,
how can he love God
whom he has not seen?   And
this commandment
we have from Him: that
he who loves God
must love his brother also.   But
whoever keeps His word,
truly the love of God
is perfected in him.
By this we know   that
we are in Him.
1 Jn. 4:20,21; 2:5

16.   1 John 4:20,21; 2:5
I s s,   I l G,   a
h h b,
h i a l;
f h w d n
l h b
w h h s,
h c h l G
w h h n s?   A
t c
w h f H: t
h w l G
m l h b a.   B
w k H w,
t t l o G
i p i h.
B t w k   t
w a i H.
Addr._____

17.   1 Peter 2:23
[Christ] **who**, when He was reviled,
did not revile in return;
when He suffered,
He did not threaten,   but
committed Himself
to Him [Father God]
who judges righteously;
1 Pet. 2:23

17.   1 Peter 2:23
w, w H w r,
d n r i r;
w H s,
H d n t,   b
c H
t H
w j r;
Addr._____

18.   1 Peter 2:21,22
For to this you were called,
because
Christ also suffered for us,
leaving us an example,   that
you should follow His steps:
Who committed no sin,
Nor was deceit found
in His mouth;
1 Pet. 2:21,22

18.   1 Peter 2:21,22
F t t y w c,
b
C a s f u,
l u a e,   t
y s f H s:
W c n s,
N w d f
i H m;
Addr._____

19. 2 Corinthians 5:20	19. 2 Corinthians 5:20
Now then,	N t,
we are ambassadors	w a a
for Christ ...	f C ...
as though God were pleading	a t G w p
through us:	t u:
we implore you	w i y
on Christ's behalf,	o C's b,
be reconciled to God.	b r t G.
2 Cor. 5:20	Addr._____

20. 2 Corinthians 5:18	20. 2 Corinthians 5:18
Now all things are of God,	N a t a o G,
who has reconciled us	w h r u
to Himself	t H
through Jesus Christ, and	t J C, a
has given us the ministry	h g u t m
of reconciliation,	o r,
2 Cor. 5:18	Addr._____

21. Romans 12:14,16,17a,19	21. Romans 12:14,16,17a,19
Bless those who persecute you;	B t w p y;
bless and do not curse.	b a d n c.
Be of the same mind	B o t s m
toward one another.	t o a.
Do not set your mind	D n s y m
on high things, but	o h t, b
associate with	a w
the humble.	t h.
Do not be wise	D n b w
in your own opinion.	i y o o.
Repay no one	R n o
evil for evil.	e f e.
Beloved, do not	B, d n
avenge yourselves, but	a y, b
rather give place to wrath;	r g p t w;
for it is written,	f i i w,
Vengeance is Mine,	V i M,
I will repay, says the Lord.	I w r, s t L.
Rom. 12:14,16,17a,19	Addr._____

22.   Romans 12:20a
Therefore [says the Lord]
If your enemy is hungry,
feed him;
If he is thirsty,
give him a drink;
Rom. 12:20a

22.   Romans 12:20a
T
I y e i h,
f h;
I h i t,
g h a d;
Addr._____

23.   Matthew 7:14b
narrow is the gate   and
difficult is the way
which leads to life,   and
there are few
who find it.
Mt. 7:14b

23.   Matthew 7:14b
n i t g   a
d i t w
w l t l, a
t a f
w f i.
Addr._____

24.   Genesis 1:21
So God created
great sea creatures   and
every living thing   that moves,
with which
the waters abounded,
according to their kind,   and
every winged bird
according to its kind.
And God saw that it was good.
Gen. 1:21

24.   Genesis 1:21
S G c
g s c   a
e l t   t m,
w w
t w a,
a t t k, a
e w b
a t i k.
A G s t i w g.
Addr._____

25.   Genesis 1:22,23
And God blessed them,
saying,
Be fruitful   and
multiply,   and
fill the waters in the seas, and
let birds multiply
on the earth.
So the evening   and
the morning
were the fifth day.
Gen. 1:22,23

25.   Genesis 1:22,23
A G b t,
s,
B f   a
m,   a
f t w i t s, a
l b m
o t e.
S t e   a
t m
w t f d.
Addr._____

DAY SIX: ANALOGY SYNOPSIS

On Creation Day Six,
God's work in Creation was to create land animals –
cattle for domesticated animals, beast for wild animals,
and "creeping thing." In His image, God created
man – male and female. God presents to Adam, Eve,
his bride.

This reminds me of Christ creating His bride – the church
of sheep from every nation; but beforehand as the Lord
forewarned, deceiving wolves and "that old serpent"
will stir up self-worship among the sheep. Faithful sheep,
living out the two greatest commandments – of trusting
unreservedly in the Lord, and secondly, sharing His
reconciling love – will be ready when the Bridegroom
comes – Rev. 3:7-13. Jesus Christ will present to Himself
His bride.

ANALOGY: CREATION DAY SIX

Analogy: a partial likeness between two things that are compared. This analogy seeks to view the Scriptures about Jesus and the church through the narrative of Genesis Chapter One.

Creation Day 6: Genesis 1:24-31

24 Then God said, "Let the earth bring forth the living creature according to its kind: cattle and creeping thing and beast of the earth, each according to its kind"; and it was so. 25 And God made the beast of the earth according to its kind, cattle according to its kind, and everything that creeps on the earth according to its kind. And God saw that it was good. 26 Then God said, "Let Us make man in Our image, according to Our likeness; let them have dominion over the fish of the sea, over the birds of the air, and over the cattle, over all the earth and over every creeping thing that creeps on the earth." 27 So God created man in His own image; in the image of God He created him; male and female He created them. 28 Then God blessed them, and God said to them, "Be fruitful and multiply; fill the earth and subdue it; have dominion over the fish of the sea, over the birds of the air, and over every living thing that moves on the earth."29 And God said, "See, I have given you every herb that yields seed which is on the face of all the earth, and every tree whose fruit yields seed; to you it shall be for food. 30 Also, to every beast of the earth, to every bird of the air, and to everything that creeps on the earth, in which there is life, I have given every green herb for food"; and it was so. 31 Then God saw everything that He had made, and indeed it was very good. So the evening and the morning were the sixth day.

God's Work in Creation:	God created land animals: domesticated and wild animals, and creeping things. In His own image, God created man – male and female.
Jesus' Work on Earth:	Marriage: The church is awaiting her Bridegroom. Jesus forewarned about false prophets and false teachers deceiving many in the last days.
Bible Verse Keywords:	Cattle; creeping thing; beast; sheep in the midst of wolves; false prophets ... in sheep's clothing; ravenous wolves; abundance of his heart; your words; mercy triumphs over judgement; why do you call me, Lord; beware of the leaven of the Pharisees; good shepherd; gives His life for the sheep; God created man in His own image; male and female; two shall become one flesh; cherishes; as the Lord does the church; married to ... Him; Christ also loved the church; gave Himself for her; a king arranged a marriage.
Pondered:	1. Land animals such as sheep, wolves, and serpent are created. Jesus said that in the last days, Satan, "that serpent of old," will deceive many, and so will wolves masquerading as sheep. Ever since the beautiful and anointed angel, Lucifer, later called Satan, measured and compared his self as best, one's eternity concludes on Christ's Lordship or fatal self-worship. True Christ-followers reject the satanic spirit of exalting self which poisoned a third of the holy angels, all earth, and for a time the Early Church.
	2. Adam and Eve, Christ and His bride – each one flesh.
	3. Could it be that some land animals bring to mind how Satan and false teachers deceive, while Adam and Eve are a typology of the Lord Jesus Christ marrying His bride – the church of sheep from every nation?

1.   Genesis 1:24
Then God said,
Let the earth bring forth
the living creature according to its kind:
cattle   and
creeping thing   and
beast of the earth,
each according to its kind;   and
it was so.
Gen. 1:24

1.   Genesis 1:24
T G s,
L t e b f
t l c a t i k:
c   a
c t   a
b o t e,
e a t i k; a
i w s.
Addr._____

2.   Matthew 10:16; 7:15,16a
Behold, I [Jesus] send you out
as sheep
in the midst of wolves.
Therefore be wise as serpents   and
harmless as doves.
Beware of false prophets,
who come to you   in sheep's clothing, but
inwardly they are   ravenous wolves.
You will know them   by their fruits.
Mt. 10:16; 7:15,16a

2.   Matthew 10:16; 7:15,16a
B, I s y o
a s
i t m o w.
T b w a s   a
h a d.
B o f p,
w c t y   i s's c,   b
i t a   r w.
Y w k t   b t f.
Addr._____

3.   Luke 6:44a,45b; Matthew 12:36,37
For every tree is known
by its own fruit.
For out of the abundance
of the heart
his mouth speaks.   Matthew 12:36,37

But I [Jesus] say to you   that
for every idle word
men may speak,
they will give account of it
in the day of judgment.
For by your words
you will be justified,   and
by your words
you will be condemned.
Lk. 6:44a,45b; Mt.12:36,37

3.   Luke 6:44a,45b; Matthew 12:36,37
F e t i k
b i o f.
F o o t a
o t h
h m s.

B I s t y   t
f e i w
m m s,
t w g a o i
i t d o j.
F b y w
y w b j,   a
b y w
y w b c.
Addr._____

4.   Hebrews 13:15,16
Therefore by Him
let us continually offer
the sacrifice of praise to God,   that is,
the fruit of our lips,
giving thanks to His name.   But
do not forget to do good   and
to share,
for with such sacrifices
God is well pleased.
Heb. 13:15,16

4.   Hebrews 13:15,16
T b H
l u c o
t s o p t G,   t i,
t f o o l,
g t t H n.   B
d n f t d g   a
t s,
f w s s
G i w p.
Addr._____

5.   Matthew 25:31,33-37a,40
When the Son of Man comes
in His glory ...
then He will sit on the throne
of His glory.   And
He will set the sheep
on His right hand,   but
the goats on the left.
Then the King will say
to those on His right hand,
Come, you blessed of My Father,
inherit the kingdom prepared for you
from the foundation of the world:
for I was hungry   and you gave Me food;
I was thirsty   and you gave Me drink;
I was a stranger   and you took Me in;
I was naked   and you clothed Me;
I was sick   and you visited Me;
I was in prison   and you came to Me.
Then the righteous will answer Him, saying, Lord,
when did we see You ... And
the King will answer   and
say to them,
Assuredly, I say to you,
inasmuch as you did it to one
of the least of these
My brethren, you did it to Me.
Mt. 25:31,33-37a,40

5.   Matthew 25:31,33-37a,40
W t S o M c
i H g ...
t H w s o t t
o H g.   A
H w s t s
o H r h,   b
t g o t l.
T t K w s
t t o H r h,
C, y b o M F,
i t k p f y
f t f o t w:
f I w h   a y g M f;
I w t   a y g M d;
I w a s   a y t M i;
I w n   a y c M;
I w s   a y v M;
I w i p   a y c t M.
T t r w a H, s, L,
w d w s Y ... A
t K w a   a
s t t,
A, I s t y,
i a y d i t o
o t l o t
M b, y d i t M.
Addr._____

6.   James 2:13, Luke 6:36,46
For judgment is without mercy
to the one
who has shown no mercy.
Mercy triumphs over judgment. Luke 6:36,46
Therefore be merciful,
just as your Father also is merciful.   But
why do you call Me
Lord, Lord,   and
not do the things which I say?
Js. 2:13, Lk. 6:36,46

7.   Luke 12:1b-3
He began to say to His disciples
first of all,
Beware of the leaven
of the Pharisees,
which is hypocrisy.
For there is nothing covered   that
will not be revealed,   nor
hidden that will not be known.
Therefore whatever you have spoken
in the dark
will be heard in the light,   and
what you have spoken
in the ear in inner rooms
will be proclaimed on the housetops.
Lk. 12:1b-3

8.   Matthew 7:12,13
Therefore, whatever you want men
to do to you,   do also to them,
for this is the Law   and the Prophets.
Enter through the narrow gate.
For wide is the gate   and
broad is the road   that
leads to destruction,   and
there are many
who go in by it.
Mt. 7:12,13

6.   James 2:13, Luke 6:36,46
F j i w m
t t o
w h s n m.
M t o j.
T b m,
j a y F a i m. B
w d y c M
L, L,   a
n d t t w I s?
Addr._____

7.   Luke 12:1b-3
H b t s t H d
f o a,
B o t l
o t P,
w i h.
F t i n c   t
w n b r,   n
h t w n b k.
T w y h s
i t d
w b h i t l, a
w y h s
i t e i i r
w b p o t h.
Addr._____

8.   Matthew 7:12,13
T, w y w m
t d t y,   d a t t,
f t i t L   a t P.
E t t n g.
F w i t g   a
b i t r   t
l t d,   a
t a m
w g i b i.
Addr._____

9.   John 10:7b,11,14b,15b
Most assuredly, I say to you,
I am the door of the sheep
I am the good shepherd.
The good shepherd
gives His life   for the sheep ...
I know My sheep,   and
I am known by My own ...
I lay down My life   for the sheep.
Jn. 10:7b,11,14b,15b

9.   John 10:7b,11,14b,15b
M a , I s t y ,
I a t d o t s
I a t g s .
T g s
g H l   f t s ...
I k M s ,   a
a k b M o ...
I l d M l   f t s .
Addr._____

10.   Matthew 7:14b
narrow is the gate   and
difficult is the way
which leads to life,   and
there are few
who find it.
Mt. 7:14b

10.   Matthew 7:14b
n i t g   a
d i t w
w l t l ,   a
t a f
w f i .
Addr._____

11.   Genesis 1:25
And God made the beast of the earth
according to its kind,
cattle according to its kind,   and
everything that creeps on the earth
according to its kind.
And God saw that it was good.
Gen. 1:25

11.   Genesis 1:25
A G m t b o t e
a t i k ,
c a t i k ,   a
e t c o t e
a t i k .
A G s t i w g .
Addr._____

12.   Genesis 1:26
Then God said,
Let Us make man in   Our image,
according to   Our likeness;
let them have dominion
over the fish of the sea,
over the birds of the air,   and
over the cattle,
over all the earth   and
over every creeping thing   that
creeps on the earth.
Gen. 1:26

12.   Genesis 1:26
T G s ,
L U m m i   O i ,
a t   O l ;
l t h d
o t f o t s ,
o t b o t a ,   a
o t c ,
o a t e   a
o e c t   t
c o t e .
Addr._____

13.   Genesis 1:27; 2:24
So God created man   in His own image;
in the image of God   He created him;
male and female   He created them. Genesis 2:24
Therefore a man shall leave
his father and mother   and
be joined to his wife,   and
they shall become one flesh.
Gen. 1:27; 2:24

13.   Genesis 1:27; 2:24
S G c m   i H o i;
i t i o G   H c h;
m a f   H c t.
T a m s l
h f a m   a
b j t h w,   a
t s b o f.
Addr._____

14.   Ephesians 5:31,32
For this reason a man shall leave
his father and mother   and
be joined to his wife,   and
the two shall become one flesh.
This is a great mystery,   but
I speak concerning
Christ and the church.
Eph. 5:31,32

14.   Ephesians 5:31,32
F t r a m s l
h f a m   a
b j t h w,   a
t t s b o f.
T i a g m,   b
I s c
C a t c.
Addr._____

15.   Ephesians 5:29,30
For no one ever hated
his own flesh,   but
nourishes and cherishes it,
just as the Lord does the church.
For we are members
of His body,
of His flesh   and
of His bones.
Eph. 5:29,30

15.   Ephesians 5:29,30
F n o e h
h o f,   b
n a c i,
j a t L d t c.
F w a m
o H b,
o H f   a
o H b.
Addr._____

16.   Romans 7:4
Therefore, my brethren,
you also have become   dead to the law
through the body of Christ,   that
you may be married to another –
to Him
who was raised from the dead,   that
we should bear fruit to God.
Rom. 7:4

16.   Romans 7:4
T, m b,
y a h b   d t t l
t t b o C,   t
y m b m t a –
t H
w w r f t d,   t
w s b f t G.
Addr._____

17.   Ephesians 5:25b-27

Christ also loved the church   and
gave Himself for her,   that
He might sanctify   and cleanse her
with the washing of water by the word,   that
He might present her to Himself
a glorious church, not having spot   or
wrinkle or any such thing,   but that
she should be holy   and without blemish.
Eph. 5:25b-27

17.   Ephesians 5:25b-27

C a l t c   a
g H f h,   t
H m s   a c h
w t w o w b t w,   t
H m p h t H
a g c, n h s   o
w o a s t,   b t
s s b h   a w b.
Addr._____

18.   Matthew 22:2,8,10-12a

The kingdom of heaven is like a certain king
who arranged a marriage for his son ...
Then he said to his servants,
The wedding is ready,   but
those who were invited   were not worthy.
So those servants went out
into the highways   and
gathered together all   whom they found,
both bad and good.   And
the wedding hall was filled with guests. But
when the king came in to see the guests,
he saw a man there   who did not have on
a wedding garment.   So he said to him,
Friend, how did you come in here
without a wedding garment?
Mt. 22:2,8,10-12a

18.   Matthew 22:2,8,10-12a

T k o h i l a c k
w a a m f h s ...
T h s t h s,
T w i r,   b
t w w i   w n w.
S t s w o
i t h   a
g t a   w t f,
b b a g.   A
t w h w f w g.   B
w t k c i t s t g,
h s a m t   w d n h o
a w g.   S h s t h,
F, h d y c i h
w a w g?
Addr._____

19.   1 Corinthians 1:29,30

that no flesh should glory
in His presence.   But
of Him
you are in Christ Jesus,
who became for us
wisdom from God –   and
righteousness   and
sanctification   and
redemption –
1 Cor. 1:29,30

19.   1 Corinthians 1:29,30

t n f s g
i H p.   B
o H
y a i C J,
w b f u
w f G –   a
r   a
s   a
r –
Addr._____

20.   Matthew 25:1,5-10
Then the kingdom of heaven shall be likened
to ten virgins who took their lamps   and
went out to meet the bridegroom.   But
while the bridegroom was delayed,
they all slumbered and slept.   And
at midnight a cry was heard:
Behold, the bridegroom is coming;
go out to meet him!
Then all those virgins arose ...   And
the foolish said to the wise [who had oil with them]
Give us some of your oil ...
for our lamps are going out.
No, they [the wise] replied,
there may not be enough ...   And
while they [the foolish] went to buy,
the bridegroom came,   and
those who were ready
went in with him to the wedding;   and
the door was shut.
Mt. 25:1,5-10

20.   Matthew 25:1,5-10
T t k o h s b l
t t v w t t l   a
w o t m t b.   B
w t b w d,
t a s a s.   A
a m a c w h:
B, t b i c;
g o t m h!
T a t v a ...   A
t f s t t w
G u s o y o ...
f o l a g o.
N, t r,
t m n b e ...   A
w t w t b,
t b c,   a
t w w r
w i w h t t w;   a
t d w s.
Addr._____

21.   Luke 10:25,26a,29-34a,36,37
... a certain lawyer ... tested Him [Jesus], saying,
Teacher, what shall I do to inherit eternal life?
[Jesus] He said to him, What is written in the law? ...
But he, wanting to justify himself [quoted the two
greatest commandments and], said to Jesus, And
who is my neighbor? ...
Jesus answered ...   a certain priest ... passed by ...
Likewise a Levite ... passed by ...   Luke 10:30b,33
a certain man ...   wounded ... and ... half dead ...
a certain Samaritan, came where he was.   And
when he saw him,   he had compassion ...   and
took care of him ... [Jesus asked the lawyer]
So which of these three ...were a neighbor to him ...?
And he said, He who showed mercy on him.
Then Jesus said to him [the lawyer],
Go and do likewise.
Lk. 10:25,26a,29-34a,36,37

21.   Luke 10:25,26a,29-34a,36,37
... a c l ...t H, s,
T, w s I d t i e l?
H s t h, W i w i t l? ...
B h, w t j h,
s t J,   A
w i m n? ...
J a ...   a c p ... p b ...
L a L ... p b ...
a c m ... w ... a ... h d ...
a c S,   c w h w.   A
w h s h, h h c ...   a
t c o h ...
S w o t t ... w a n t h ...?
A h s, H w s m o h.
T J s t h,
G a d l.
Addr._____

22.   Galatians 3:1,3
O foolish Galatians!
Who has bewitched you   that
you should   not obey the truth,
before whose eyes
Jesus Christ was clearly portrayed among you
as crucified? ...
Are you so foolish?
Having begun in the Spirit,
are you now being made perfect
by the flesh?
Gal. 3:1,3

22.   Galatians 3:1,3
O f G!
W h b y   t
y s   n o t t,
b w e
J C w c p a y
a c? ...
A y s f?
H b i t S,
a y n b m p
b t f?
Addr._____

23.   1 Corinthians 15:50,51
Now this I say, brethren, that
flesh and blood cannot inherit
the kingdom of God;   nor
does corruption inherit incorruption.
Behold, I tell you a mystery:
We shall not all sleep,   but
we shall all be changed –
1 Cor. 15:50,51

23.   1 Corinthians 15:50,51
N t I s, b,   t
f a b c i
t k o G;   n
d c i i.
B, I t y a m:
W s n a s,   b
w s a b c –
Addr._____

24.   Matthew 25:13
Watch therefore,   for you know neither
the day nor the hour   in which the Son of Man
is coming.
Mt. 25:13

24.   Matthew 25:13
W t,   f y k n
t d n t h   i w t S o M
i c.
Addr._____

25.   Genesis 1:28
Then God blessed them, and
God said to them,
Be fruitful   and multiply;
fill the earth   and subdue it;
have dominion
over the fish of the sea,
over the birds of the air, and
over every living thing   that
moves on the earth.
Gen. 1:28

25.   Genesis 1:28
T G b t,   a
G s t t,
B f   a m;
f t e   a s i;
h d
o t f o t s,
o t b o t a,   a
o e l t   t
m o t e.
Addr._____

26.   Genesis 1:29,30
And God said,   See, I have given you
every herb   that yields seed
which is on the face
of all the earth,   and
every tree   whose fruit yields seed;
to you   it shall be for food.
Also, to every beast of the earth,
to every bird of the air,   and
to everything   that creeps on the earth,
in which there is life,
I have given   every green herb
for food;   and it was so.
Gen 1:29,30

26.   Genesis 1:29,30
A G s,   S, I h g y
e h   t y s
w i o t f
o a t e,   a
e t   w f y s;
t y   i s b f f.
A, t e b o t e,
t e b o t a,   a
t e   t c o t e,
i w t i l,
I h g   e g h
f f;   a i w s.
Addr._____

27.   John 6:51
[Jesus said] I am the living bread ...   and
the bread   that
I ... give is My flesh,
which I ... give
for the life
of the world.
Jn. 6:51

27.   John 6:51
I a t l b ... a
t b   t
I ... g i M f,
w I ... g
f t l
o t w.
Addr._____

28.   John 12:26
If anyone serves Me,
let him   follow Me;   and
where I am,
there My servant will be also.
If anyone serves Me,
him My Father will honor.
Jn. 12:26

28.   John 12:26
I a s M,
l h   f M;   a
w I a,
t M s w b a.
I a s M,
h M F w h.
Addr._____

29.   Genesis 1:31
Then God saw everything   that
He had made,   and indeed
it was very good.
So the evening   and the morning
were the sixth day.
Gen. 1:31

29.   Genesis 1:31
T G s e   t
H h m,   a i
i w v g.
S t e   a t m
w t s d.
Addr._____

DAY SEVEN: ANALOGY SYNOPSIS

On Day Seven,
God rested from His work. Creation is finished.
God blessed the seventh day and sanctified it.

This reminds me that Jesus rested from His work;
the sacrifice is finished. He blessed the whole world
for He secured "the way" of direct access to Holy
God, and the sanctification of His disciples.

Jesus Christ glorified His Father on earth, and in
heaven Father God glorified His Son – the victorious
Lamb – the true Light.

ANALOGY: GOD RESTED

God's Work of Creation Is Finished.   Jesus' Work, to Die to Save Sinners, Is Finished; He Lives.

Day 7: Genesis 2:1-3

1 Thus the heavens and the earth, and all the host of them, were finished. 2 And on the seventh day God ended His work which He had done, and He rested on the seventh day from all His work which He had done. 3 Then God blessed the seventh day and sanctified it, because in it He rested from all His work which God had created and made.

God's Work in Creation: Done: God is finished. He rested on the seventh day.

Jesus' Work on Earth: Done: Jesus Christ is finished; He died on the cross for our sins and paid our penalty of death – once for all. Before His crucifixion, Jesus secured from His Father, the perfect Counselor and Helper for His disciples – the Holy Spirit. Thereby once resurrected, the Lord Jesus Christ sat down at His Father's right hand – at rest from His atoning work on earth.

Bible Verse Keywords: The heavens and the earth ... were finished; seventh day God ended His work; He rested; He said, It is finished; rose early on the first day of the week; He was received up in heaven; sat down at the right hand of God.

Pondered: 1. The heavens and the earth were finished, and God rested from all His work. He blessed the seventh day and sanctified it. The sentence of death for every man, woman, and child was paid; "It is finished." Jesus is at rest from all His sacrificial, substitutionary work.

2. Hebrews10:14 says, "For by one offering He has perfected forever those who are being sanctified." "Christ also loved the church and gave Himself for her, that He might sanctify and cleanse her with the washing of water by the word," declares Ephesians 5:25b,26. Jesus, Who knew no sin, bore our sins, so we might become His righteousness before His Holy Father.

3. Jesus said to His Father in John 17:4,5, **"I have glorified You on the earth. I have finished the work which You have given Me to do. And now, O Father, glorify Me together with Yourself, with the glory which I had with You before the world was."**

4. Thus the resurrected Jesus Christ was carried up to heaven and received by His Father. Christ sat down at His Father's right hand.

5. With the return of His Son – the victorious Mediator, God sent the Holy Spirit – the Counselor Helper. Now He is at work on earth drawing people to Jesus, indwelling believers, sanctifying and filling them, speaking and teaching of Christ, and empowering disciples to be like their Savior Lord.

6. The Lord Jesus Christ is at work in heaven preparing a place for each disciple transformed by His finished cross work and His Lordship.

1.   Genesis 2:1-3
Thus the heavens and the earth,   and
all the host of them,
were finished.   And
on the seventh day
God ended His work
which He had done,   and
He rested on the seventh day
from all His work
which He had done.

Then God blessed the seventh day   and
sanctified it,
because in it He rested
from all His work
which God had created   and made.
Gen. 2:1-3

1.   Genesis 2:1-3
T t h a t e, a
a t h o t,
w f.   A
o t s d
G e H w
w H h d,   a
H r o t s d
f a H w
w H h d.

T G b t s d   a
s i,
b i i H r
f a H w
w G h c   a m.
Addr._____

2.   John 19:28a,30b; Luke 23:46b
After this, Jesus,
knowing that all things
were now accomplished,   that
the Scripture might be fulfilled ...
He said, It is finished! ... Luke 23:46b
He breathe His last.
Jn. 19:28a,30b; Lk. 23:46b

2.   John 19:28a,30b; Luke 23:46b
A t, J,
k t a t
w n a, t
t S m b f ...
H s, I i f ! ...
H b H l.
Addr._____

3.   Mark 16:9a,14a,19b; Luke 24:50b,51
He rose early
on the first day of the week ...
Later He appeared to the eleven ... Luke 24:50b,51
He lifted up His hands   and blessed them.
Now it came to pass,
while He blessed them ...
He was parted from them   and
carried up into heaven. Mark 16:19b
He was received up in heaven, and
sat down
at the right hand of God.
Mk. 16:9a,14a,19b; Lk. 24:50b,51

3.   Mark 16:9a,14a,19b; Luke 24:50b,51
H r e
o t f d o t w ...
L H a t t e ...
H l u H h   a b t.
N i c t p,
w H b t ...
H w p f t   a
c u i h.
H w r u i h, a
s d
a t r h o G.
Addr._____

4.   Colossians 1:19,20
For it pleased the Father   that
in Him [Jesus] all the fullness
should dwell,   and
by Him to reconcile all things to Himself ...
whether things on earth   or
things in heaven,
having made peace
through the blood of His cross.
Col. 1:19,20

4.   Colossians 1:19,20
F i p t F   t
i H a t f
s d,   a
b H t r a t t H ...
w t o e   o
t i h,
h m p
t t b o H c.
Addr._____

5.   1 Timothy 2:5,6a
For there is one God   and
one Mediator between God   and men,
the Man Christ Jesus,
who gave Himself
a ransom for all
1 Tim. 2:5,6a

5.   1 Timothy 2:5,6a
F t i o G   a
o M b G   a m,
t M C J,
w g H
a r f a
Addr._____

6.   1 Peter 1:3,4
Blessed be the God   and
Father of our Lord Jesus Christ,
who according to His abundant mercy
has begotten us again
to a living hope
through the resurrection of Jesus Christ
from the dead,
to an inheritance incorruptible   and
undefiled   and that
does not fade away,
reserved in heaven for you.
1 Pet. 1:3,4

6.   1 Peter 1:3,4
B b t G   a
F o o L J C,
w a t H a m
h b u a
t a l h
t t r o J C
f t d,
t a i i   a
u   a t
d n f a,
r i h f y.
Addr._____

7.   1 John 4:9
In this the love of God
was manifested toward us,   that
God has sent His only begotten Son
into the world,   that
we might live through Him.
1 Jn. 4:9

7.   1 John 4:9
I t t l o G
w m t u,   t
G h s H o b S
i t w,   t
w m l t H.
Addr._____

8.   Romans 15:13
Now may the God of hope
fill you with all joy   and
peace in believing,   that
you may abound in hope
by the power of the Holy Spirit.
Rom. 15:13

8.   Romans 15:13
N m t G o h
f y w a j   a
p i b,   t
y m a i h
b t p o t H S.
Addr._____

9.   Romans 1:20a
For since the creation   of the world
His invisible attributes   are clearly seen,
being understood by the things   that
are made,
even His eternal power   and
Godhead ...
Rom. 1:20a

9.   Romans 1:20a
F s t c   o t w
H i a   a c s,
b u b t t   t
a m,
e H e p   a
G ...
Addr._____

10.   John 1:9
That was the true Light
which gives light
to every man
coming into the world.
Jn. 1:9

10.   John 1:9
T w t t L
w g l
t e m
c i t w.
Addr._____

11.   Revelation 21:2
Then I, [Apostle] John, saw
the holy city, New Jerusalem,
coming down out of heaven from God,
prepared as a bride
adorned for her **husband**.
Rev. 21:2

11.   Revelation 21:2
T I, J, s
t h c, N J,
c d o o h f G,
p a a b
a f h **h**.
Addr._____

12.   Revelation 21:23
The city had no need
of the sun   or
of the moon to shine in it,
for the glory of God
illuminated it.
The Lamb is its light.
Rev. 21:23

12.   Revelation 21:23
T c h n n
o t s   o
o t m t s i i,
f t g o G
i i.
T L i i l.
Addr._____

EPILOGUE: THE ESSENTIALS

HOW TO BE SAVED / RECEIVE CHRIST IN YOUR HEART

Holy God Creator,

I, _____, on _____ __, 2____.
    (name)   (date)

Admit that I am a sinner, and I deserve Your penalty of death for sin. I am sorry for my sins, and sincerely ask you to forgive me.

I:

Believe that Jesus Christ is Your Son and God. He paid my penalty of death when He died on the cross for my sins. He rose on the third day; therefore, I am assured that the penalty for my sin was paid and accepted. My forgiveness is only through faith in Jesus' sacrifice for me.

I:

Confess that I have received Your gift of forgiveness, and desire You to control my life. Now I am *a child of God.* I am an imitator of Jesus Christ empowered by God to turn away from sin and live victoriously for Christ. I am *a believer, saved, an heir of God with eternal life.* **Now Jesus Christ is my Lord, Master, and Savior.**

LORDSHIP: TWO GREATEST COMMANDMENTS

Jesus answered ...

you shall love the Lord your God

with all your heart,

with all your soul,

with all your mind, and

with all your strength.

This is the first commandment.

And the second, like it, is this:

You shall love your neighbor

as yourself.

There is no other commandment

greater than these.

Mark 12:29-31

THE HOLY BIBLE: THE LIVING WORD OF GOD

For the word of God is living and powerful, and sharper than any two-edged sword, piercing even to the division of soul and spirit, and of joints and marrow, and is a discerner of the thoughts and intents of the heart. And there is no creature hidden from His sight, but all things are naked and open to the eyes of Him to whom we must give account. Hebrews 4:12,13

If in reading this book, you prayed and received Jesus Christ into your heart as your Savior and Lord, please tell us.